lotte's country kitchen

To Daisy
The most beautiful, funny, bright,
kind and glorious daughter
anyone could wish for.

In memory of my Mum
A rather splendid cook

And in memory of two gorgeous, fun-
loving, foodie women and dear friends,
Slavka Bradley and Margaret Browne.
taken too bloody early to cancer.

*'This is the season for fine wines,
laughter, roses and **drunken** friends.
Enjoy this moment, for this moment
is your life'*
Omar Khayyam

lotte's country kitchen

Lotte Duncan

A.

First published in Great Britain in 2010
by **Absolute Press**
Scarborough House
29 James Street West
Bath BA1 2BT
Phone 44 (0) 1225 316013
Fax 44 (0) 1225 445836
E-mail info@absolutepress.co.uk
Website www.absolutepress.co.uk

Text copyright
Lotte Duncan
Photography copyright
Lara Holmes

Publisher Jon Croft
Commissioning Editor
Meg Avent
Editor Jane Bamforth
Art Direction and Design
Matt Inwood and Claire Siggery
Publishing Assistant
Andrea O'Connor
Photographer Lara Holmes
Food Styling Lotte Duncan

www.lotteduncan.com

A catalogue record of this book is
available from the British Library.

ISBN 9781906650285

Printed and bound in Spain by
Graficas 94.

A note about the text
This book was set using the fonts
Century and Angelic Warfare.
The first Century typeface was cut
in 1894. In 1975 an updated family of
Century typefaces was designed by
Tony Stan for ITC. Angelic Warfare is a
beautifully extravagant serif font
created by Andrew Hart with, as he
describes it, 'lots of lines, artistic
elegance and love' His collection of
stunning contemporary faces can be
found at www.dirt2.com.

contents

introduction

When people enter my cottage and sit at my table they know very well that there is little chance they'll be able to move with any great speed after the meal.

It is well known that I like to feed people enormously and that all the food eaten in my kitchen is in fact void of any calories. See it as a neutral zone where no food is fattening, no weight will be gained and only lovely things will happen to you if you eat it. It's true. Honest.

I just want people to enjoy themselves and eat with a smile on their face, embracing all that is good about the recipes that form the backbone of my life. I look at food in a very simple way. It has to be easy to cook, look pretty and taste yummy. That's it.

Most people want to be able to prepare a delicious meal in their own home that doesn't involve 15 saucepans, a brigade of chefs and expensive, difficult to source ingredients. A recipe shouldn't need a cooking thesaurus to decipher it.

I've been to people's houses for dinner, (yes, sometimes I do get invited – but I have to behave myself) and often the host is so tired from cooking the meal that they are face down, asleep at the table from exhaustion. Either that or they have passed out – you can never be quite sure.

I believe that to enjoy your food, you don't want to be so tired from cooking, that you're unable to lift a fork to eat it. The process of cooking a recipe should be just as enjoyable as eating it.

As far back as I can remember, I have thought of nothing else but food. When my parents came back from an evening out, they had to regale me with what they had eaten, why they had chosen it and what they had thought. Bless them for being so patient – I can only guess at how irritating that interrogation must have been!

Early cooking was ... interesting to say the least. My mother was extremely generous with her kitchen and allowed me to spend many hours in there making a hideous mess. I still recall pretending to talk to an audience or indeed a camera. I obviously had a precocious longing for media attention even then!

As a child, my initial recipe writing was simple, yet frightful. The title of a dish was mulled over for a few days until pen was put to paper. Then with great aplomb I would announce its name with colossal seriousness and a hint of nonchalance, to people trying very hard not to laugh loudly, and possibly hysterically, at my clumsy attempts at cookery literature.

My first recipe was called Pineapple Flanky – a stack of flaccid pancakes, sandwiched together with evaporated cream and canned pineapple slices. Yes, I am fully aware that this award-winning combination was indeed a dreadful mishmash of ideas, but it was the 70s and canned pineapple was the height of sophistication at the time... apparently!

Luckily I've got a bit better, and as much as I would like to write a book of one hundred things to do with canned pineapple, I've decided instead to give you my favourite recipes. These are the dishes that I've been stuffing down the faces of my family and friends for years. And now it's your turn.

before you start...

There are just a few things I need to tell you before you embark on this book. Nothing complicated, because none of my recipes are. All of the ingredients I use are easily available and you shouldn't have to search high and low for them. However, below are a few favourite things that I've picked out and where to find them.

Rapeseed oil

Rapeseed oil is absolutely delicious and I can't believe I only started using it a few years ago. My favourite is Wharfe Valley Extra Virgin from Yorkshire. The Kilby family who run the farm where it's made are so lovely and the taste of this particular rapeseed hooked me from day one. They sell it oak-smoked, chilli and plain and they send it mail order too. Get in touch with them and order a bottle or two (*www.wharfevalleyfarms.co.uk*).

Another good reason to use rapeseed oil is the fact that it contains the lowest saturated fat content of any oil – less than half that of olive oil. It has ten times more omega 3 than olive oil and is a good source of vitamin E. Well that does if for me. That and the fact that it tastes fresh and green – somewhere between freshly picked asparagus and runner beans.

I have used olive oil, sunflower and groundnut oil in my recipes too, where I think they are best, but rapeseed is in most of my recipes. However, if you don't want or have it, then olive oil is absolutely fine to use. Just don't fry with the extra virgin.

Herbs

I love fresh herbs and use them whenever I can. I have a large garden where I can grow them, but I do know how lucky I am to have the space. I also know how bad I am at growing thyme and sage – I forget where I've planted it and then it dies! So, in my recipes, and because I actually think thyme and sage are the nicest as dried herbs, I've used them. Once you buy a pot of each, you'll soon use them up with the recipes in this book, so they won't go to waste.

Edible glitter

Yes really! Now if I had my way I'd decorate my house in it! I just love it and I think it makes cakes and puddings glorious. I buy it from A Piece of Cake in Thame, Oxfordshire. But if you can't get there, have a look at their website and you can order some. There are other places to buy it of course, but Thame is my local town. A pretty market town with lots of lovely independent food shops too. *www.apieceofcakethame.co.uk*.

Sausages

Musk's sausages are in my opinion the most delicious sausages around. You can buy them in most supermarkets, and you can also get them online at *www.musks.com*. Chris and Jill Sheen who run Musk's took it over a few years ago and they are just lovely, lovely people. There has been a long line of Royal patronage for Musk's and in 2005, they received a Royal Warrant from Her Majesty Queen Elizabeth II. And I'm not surprised as their Newmarket sausages, Pork and Leek and even Gluten Free are the most delicious sausages I've ever tasted. I always use Musk's for my curried sausage rolls in December.

A note on measures

I've tested these recipes using proper sized measuring spoons – you know the sort. You can use the spoons in your cutlery drawer, but they're not quite as exact and don't always match my measurements in these recipes. So if you have a moment to spare to buy some proper ones, they will make a difference, won't cost much and you'll get plenty of use out of them.

Thoughts on shopping

I'm very aware that supermarkets pack meat and other ingredients in different weight packs than I sometimes ask for in my recipes. I've tried my best to match them, but I'm also aware that not everyone shops at a supermarket. And not everyone should! What about our independent retailers? Support these people, they need it more than ever and they'll often accommodate your requests much more than a corporate machine. They'll give you the amount you need however small or large. My local butcher Tony and his wife, often weigh out a couple of rashers of bacon for older people on a pension, and he always has time to chat. Supermarket shopping, however convenient (and I do use them) is a bit moronic. We glide up and down the aisles, rarely looking around and then leave, a little poorer and perhaps not having spoken or engaged with anyone at all. Except to the cashier and all they may say is 'Card in', 'PIN number please', 'Cash back?', 'Take your card out' and finally, 'Here's your receipt'. Quite.

A word about eggs
Egg size is medium, unless I say large!

And finally....
I really do hope you enjoy reading and cooking from this book as much as I've enjoyed writing it. It's taken almost a year of my life and I've had a wonderful time doing it.

(Slight panic at the end when my computer hard drive breathed its last and I thought I'd lost it, the book that is. Yes, I now know the benefits of back up! Luckily, Robyn and Simon came up trumps and lent me their laptop and I re-did the work I'd lost when I hadn't backed up the last bit on the didgery-do-thingy-me-jig that you put in the side of the computer – USB/external hard drive perhaps? Lord knows. I have a pink computer. Why would a woman with a pink computer know anything about the technical side of things? And a big thank you to Gary at Computers, Accessories and Other Stuff in Thame – and *www.caaos.com* is the unashamed plug he so richly deserves – who managed to save it. It was touch and go and I'm sorry I was a little hysterical...)

Right, I think that's it. I'm off for a gin and a well deserved lie down – enjoy my book, it's a bit silly in places, but most of it makes sense.

Lotte
(May 2010)

11 before you start...

january

As far as I'm concerned,
as soon as December is out of
the way and Christmas packed up and
stored in the attic, spring is here...
I am known for my optimism.
Perhaps a little enthusiastic and
premature, but it's what keeps me
going through this dark, chilly month.

I find a bottle of wine
and some friends can help too.

cheeky olives

I am part of a fabulous bunch of birds in my lane and we meet every other Tuesday. We originally met for a spot of knitting, tapestry or crochet. When I first approached the girls with this idea, they weren't entirely sure.

Would they look a little silly, middle aged, daft or even... sad?

'No', I cried, 'It's cool, all the celebs are doing it, and I've just finished crocheting a large bedspread in between takes on my Dial a Mum *series on ITV. Look at me! I'm groovy, down with the kids' n'all that... innit!'*

That didn't work, so I mentioned there would be wine. Eight o'clock the following Tuesday, there they were at my door.

Having met a couple of times, I thought we should have a collective noun to describe out little cluster. Many words were thrown into the pot, but we settled on Hussy. We are now a Hussy of knitters or wine drinkers, depending on how you look at it. We each take it in turns to host the Hussy and when I host, I serve these among other nibbles.

Ignore the expensive pre-marinated olives you buy in supermarkets. Buy a cheap, large jar of green or black olives in brine. Drain them, rinse them and add the ingredients listed below. These cheeky olives have been in my fridge for many years (not the original jar, you understand!) and are often pulled out for friends. Always on hand, and even better after a time marinating in the jar, they are delicious, cheap and scrumptious. Sometimes for an extra kick, and if I have any around in my kitchen, I add some fresh chilli.

354g jar pitted, and perhaps stuffed, green olives
2 cloves garlic, crushed
grated zest and juice of 1 lemon
1 tablespoon Thai chilli dipping sauce
1 tablespoon shredded basil leaves
1 small red chilli, deseeded and chopped (optional)
2 tablespoons olive oil

Drain the olives and rinse them under cold running water. Layer them back into the jar with the garlic, lemon zest and juice, chilli sauce, basil and chilli, if using, and finally add the olive oil.

Shake the jar well and then leave the olives in the fridge for a day or so before you eat them. Although I have been known to serve them straight away, they will keep for up to 2 months in the fridge.

beef with orange and walnut, pecan and mustard dumplings

Oooh I do love a dumpling! Especially when they are crunchy and gravy soaked on the outside, and fluffy and light in the middle. This dish has been served many a time at my cookery demonstrations and been taught to all and sundry. It's always welcomed enormously and starts the dumpling debate with earnest... 'I've never had much success with my dumplings'. 'Wish I could make them like my mum did'. 'My wife's dumplings are floppy and flaccid'...OK, that's enough thank you...!

Serves 4–6

For the stew
3 tablespoons plain flour
900g/2lb diced stewing steak
4 tablespoons rapeseed oil
3 medium onions, cut into eighths, roots trimmed but left intact to hold the onions together
1 tablespoon dark brown sugar
6 celery sticks, cut into chunks
3 large carrots, cut into chunks
275ml/10fl oz red wine
grated zest and juice of 1 orange
570ml/1 pint good beef stock
1 fresh bay leaf
1/4 teaspoon dried thyme
1 tablespoon chopped fresh parsley
3 garlic cloves, crushed
salt and freshly ground black pepper

For the dumplings
350g/12oz self-raising flour
175g/6oz suet (see Lotte's tips)
3–4 tablespoons wholegrain mustard
50g/2oz walnuts, roughly chopped
50g/2oz pecan nuts, roughly chopped
steamed broccoli, to serve

Preheat the oven to 180°C/fan oven 160°C/gas mark 4. **Aga 4/3-door** *Middle of the baking oven.* **Aga 2-door** *Grid shelf on floor of roasting oven with cold plain shelf on second runners.*

For the stew, place the flour onto a large plate and season with a little salt and pepper. Toss the meat in it and shake off any excess.

Heat 3 tablespoons of the rapeseed oil in a large flameproof casserole dish. Fry and brown the beef in batches, remove and keep warm.

Add the remaining oil to the dish and cook the onions for 5 minutes. Add the brown sugar and fry for a few more minutes until the onions are browned and starting to caramelise.

Now add the celery, carrots, red wine, orange zest and juice, beef stock, herbs and garlic. Return the meat to the dish and bring the stew up to the boil. Simmer for 5 minutes then cover and place in the oven for 1½–1¾ hours or until the meat is tender. **Aga 4/3/2-door** *Place in the simmering oven and cook slowly for 3–4 hours until the meat is tender.*

Remove the stew from the oven and increase the temperature to 200°C/fan oven 180°C/gas mark 6. **Aga 4/3/2-door** *Grid shelf on the floor of the roasting oven.*

Once the meat is cooked it's time to make the dumplings. Toss the flour and suet into a large mixing bowl. Add the mustard, walnuts, pecans and seasoning and then gradually add 200–255ml/ 7–8fl oz cold water to form a firm dough.

Roll the dough into golf-ball sized dumplings and place on top of the beef. Return the stew to the oven and cook without the lid for 10 minutes. Turn the dumplings and cook for another 10 minutes until brown.

Serve the stew with the dumplings and some steamed broccoli – the colours look lovely together on the plate.

Lotte's tips
I think we all need a bit of suet in our lives. Nowadays, perhaps not so much as in the past, because we spend a large portion of our lives on our bottoms, and generally that's where suet ends up!

We don't need it to keep us warm as we have central heating. We don't need it to lay down energy reserves as we don't walk miles and ride horses as much.

However, I believe we do still need it – because it's scrumptious when in pastry or dumplings and is part of our culinary history.

Don't try to use reduced fat suet; I know it's tempting because saturated fat isn't good for us if eaten regularly. Just be a little bit naughty and cook with full fat shredded suet and just eat it a couple of times over the year. It has a better flavour and makes lighter, fluffier dumplings!

daisy's favourite steamed chocolate and almond birthday pudding

Daisy's birthday is on January 14. She has been fixated on this pudding for many years, never quite forgiving me for making it at a demonstration when she was 10 and not bringing any back for her. Motherly guilt is a strong emotion, so in an effort to redeem myself, I have named the pudding after her!

Serves 4

butter, for greasing
110g/4oz butter, softened
110g/4oz soft light brown muscovado
   sugar
2 eggs, beaten
75g/3oz dark chocolate
110g/4oz self-raising flour
50g/2oz ground almonds
2 tablespoons semi-skimmed milk
1/2 teaspoon almond extract
2 x 37g packets Maltesers
Vanilla and bay custard sauce (see
   below), to serve

Butter a 900ml/1 1/2 pint pudding basin.

Place the butter and sugar in a medium mixing bowl and cream them together with a wooden spoon until pale and fluffy. Gradually add the beaten eggs, mixing well after each addition.

Roughly break the dark chocolate into pieces and place them in a small heatproof bowl. Place the bowl over a pan of gently simmering water on the hob and stir the chocolate occasionally until it is melted.

Fold the flour and ground almonds into the creamed mixture. Stir in the milk. Place half the mixture into a separate bowl. Add the melted chocolate to one half of the mixture and stir well. Add the almond extract to the other half of the mixture and mix well.

Spoon the mixtures alternately into the greased basin, scattering over the Maltesers as you do. Smooth over the top.

Cover the bowl with a large piece of greased greaseproof paper or foil and secure it in place with string.

Half fill a steamer or large saucepan with boiling water and steam the pudding for 1 1/2–2 hours until the middle is firm to the touch. Make sure you keep an eye on the water level and top it up with boiling water at intervals if necessary.

For the Aga *Bring to the boil and steam the pudding on the simmering plate for 30 minutes. Top the steamer or pan up with boiling water, then transfer it to the simmering oven for 11/2–2 hours. The simmering oven is very kind though, so if you need to leave if for bit longer, it should be fine.*

Once the pudding is cooked, remove lit from the steamer or pan, untie the string and take off the paper or foil. Place a serving plate on top of the bowl and carefully invert it so that the pudding plops onto the plate. Serve the pudding with Vanilla and bay custard sauce.

Vanilla and bay custard sauce

This deliciously flavoured custard sauce, has an unusual taste, but goes beautifully with Daisy's favourite birthday steamed chocolate and almond pudding. Make it after the pudding has been steaming for about an hour.

It is a traditional English custard, delicate and genteel. It won't be like the thick custard you get from a can (which I love – see Bread pudding, page 187), but a custard which will spill gently over your pudding and surround it in a creamy, vanilla and bay scented puddle.

Serves 4

275ml/10fl oz semi-skimmed milk
150ml/5fl oz double cream
1/2 vanilla pod, split
1 small fresh bay leaf
3 egg yolks
1 teaspoon arrowroot
1 tablespoon light brown sugar

Pour the milk and cream into a small non-stick saucepan. Scrape the seeds out of the vanilla pod and add them, with the pod and the bay leaf to the pan. Bring up to scalding point and then set aside for the flavours to infuse for 10 minutes.

Remove the vanilla pod and bay leaf from the pan. Rinse the pod and dry then place it in a jar of spare sugar – this is great way to recycle the pod and make wonderful vanilla-infused sugar.

Beat the egg yolks, arrowroot and brown sugar together in a medium mixing bowl; pour over the infused milk and cream, and mix together thoroughly. Using the arrowroot is a Delia tip that I've followed for years – it keeps the egg yolks a little more stable and helps to prevent them curdling.

Return the milk mixture to a clean, small, non-stick saucepan. Cook, stirring, over a low heat until the sauce thickens, taking care not to let it boil or you'll end up with scrambled eggs! Just be patient and make sure you keep the heat low and take your time – it will take about 5 minutes.

Strain the sauce through a sieve to remove any tough egg white and serve it warm.

Lotte's tips
This custard also goes really well with Steamed cherry Bakewell pudding (see page 41) or Bread pudding (see page 187).

little cheesy salmon pots with marinated cucumber

Everyone has a failsafe dish that they pull out of the hat to ensure success and a low heart rate when hosting a party – be it informal or otherwise. This is mine. All prepared in advance and then popped into the oven 10 minutes before you want to eat. Perfect. I served this one year at our lane Burn's Night supper. Every year, looking for any excuse to behave badly we arrange the whole menu, including the haggis and sort out which house will host which course. This is usually done at a Hussy, over much wine and perhaps a little knitting. Oh, who am I kidding – just the wine. I can't fit 14 around my table, so this particular year Robyn and Simon offered up their house on the proviso that I cooked the starter. Fair deal I thought – I won't have to wash up. Phoebe, Dave and Sue were to host the Scottish cocktails (really, don't ask) at Sue's, which would help us find our merry way back over the road to Robyn and Simon's for the salmon pots. Haggis was to be served at Caroline and Nick's opposite and then pudding, in the form of Cranachan (using unseasonal raspberries, sorry – and please don't tell anyone) was to be the final stop at Rob and Julia's – next door. You see, not far to walk. Probably only about 15 steps each way. So how did we lose various revellers during the evening, who then re-appeared 20 minutes or so later, with no memory of where they'd been? Or indeed who they were. How did we all get into such a messy, muddy state and who on earth thought a conga the best way to travel? I'm sure all these questions wouldn't have been necessary, if we hadn't drunk the Scottish cocktails. I blame Sue.

Serves 6

For the salmon pots
butter, for greasing
225g/8oz smoked salmon
50g/2oz butter
50g/2oz flour
425ml/15fl oz semi-skimmed milk
110g/4oz Gruyère cheese, grated
1 tablespoon wholegrain mustard
1 heaped teaspoon English mustard
50g/2oz breadcrumbs

For the marinated cucumber
1 cucumber, peeled
2 tablespoons white wine vinegar
3 tablespoons clear honey
2 tablespoons chopped fresh dill
1 teaspoon fennel seeds
1 bag of mixed salad leaves
freshly ground black pepper

Butter 6 ramekins and place them on a baking tray.

To make the salmon pots, chop up the smoked salmon and divide it among the ramekins.

Melt the butter in a small, non-stick saucepan over a medium heat and add the flour. Mix together using a wooden spoon. Remove the pan from the heat and gradually add the milk, stirring continuously. Place the pan back on the heat and keep stirring until the sauce is lump-free and smooth. Simmer for 1 minute to cook the flour. The sauce is supposed to be quite thick so don't worry!

Add the cheese and mustards to the pan, stir well, and season with a little black pepper. You don't need salt as both the cheese and the salmon are salty enough. Divide the sauce between the ramekins and sprinkle over the breadcrumbs. Set aside until you are ready to cook the pots.

An hour before you are going to serve the salmon pots, make the marinated cucumber. Peel the cucumber into ribbons with a potato peeler and place in a medium bowl. Add all the remaining ingredients, except the salad leaves, and a grinding of black pepper. Set aside to marinate.

To cook the pots, preheat the oven to 220°C/fan oven 200°C/gas mark 7. **Aga 4/3/2-door** *Lower roasting oven. Place in the oven for 8–10 minutes until bubbling and golden brown.*

At the last minute, just before serving, toss the marinated cucumber with the salad and serve on plates at the side of the ramekins.

nutty treacle tart

Nutty bird makes a Nutty tart. Nuff said.

Makes one 23cm/9 inch tart

For the pastry
225g/8oz plain flour
150g/5oz butter
grated zest of 1 orange
3 tablespoons orange juice

For the filling
200g/7oz mixed nuts e.g. pecan, hazelnut and almond
3 eggs, beaten
75g/3oz butter, softened
75g/3oz soft dark brown sugar
1 teaspoon cornflour
2 tablespoons maple syrup
225g/8oz golden syrup
1 teaspoon vanilla extract

cream or ice cream and maple syrup, to serve

Preheat the oven to 200°C/fan oven 180°C/gas mark 6. **Aga 4/3/2-door** *Grid shelf on floor of roasting oven.*

Place the mixed nuts on a baking sheet and toast them in the preheated oven for 2–3 minutes. Allow the nuts to cool and then roughly chop them.

Make the pastry by putting the flour, butter and orange zest into a food processor and whizzing until it looks like breadcrumbs. Add the orange juice and pulse until it comes together. Wrap the pastry in clingfilm and chill in the fridge for 30 minutes.

Roll out the pastry on a floured worksurface and use it to line a 23cm/9-inch loose-based flan tin. Chill again, this time in the freezer for 15 minutes. Line the pastry case with greaseproof paper and baking beans and bake it blind (see Lotte's tips) in the oven for 10 minutes. **Aga 4/3/2-door** *On the bottom of the roasting oven for 10 minutes no grid shelf, then replace the grid shelf for the next stage.*

Remove the paper and the beans and then return to the oven for 2 minutes. Brush with a little of the egg for the filling, place on a baking sheet and then return again to the oven to seal for 1 minute. Remove.

Reduce the oven temperature to 180°C/fan oven 160°C/gas mark 4.

To make the filling, beat the butter and sugar together in a bowl until pale and fluffy, slowly add the beaten eggs and cornflour. Stir in the maple and golden syrup and the vanilla extract. If it looks a bit curdled, don't panic it's fine!

Stir in the toasted nuts, and then pour the filling into the pastry case.

Bake in the oven for 20 minutes. **Aga 4/3-door** *Middle of the baking oven.* **Aga 2-door** *Grid shelf on the floor of the roasting oven with the cold plain shelf on second runners.* Cover with a piece of foil and then replace in the oven for another 25–35 minutes or until the filling is just set in the middle.

Serve warm with some cream or ice cream and perhaps a little more maple syrup.

Lotte's tips
Scrunch your piece of greaseproof up a bit, you'll find it fits the flan tin better. I don't use bought baking beans made of clay – I use green lentils. I keep them in a jar for this very purpose and use them over and again – cheap to buy and they last for ages!

This tart is a rather marvellous way to use up the Christmas nuts that you buy each year with enthusiasm and then spend the rest of January regretting – the pile never seems to go down! Use them for this – any mixture of nuts will do.

roast chicken with marmalade butter

Once upon a time, there was a fabulous show called *Great Food Live*. I regularly worked on it and it was filmed in a studio, around the country and also in my cottage. It was lovely to work on, all the crew were brilliant and I made some very good friends. When you were asked to do a studio show, you'd be told the week before what the theme was going to be. It still amazes me how fresh the show was after five years of airings five days a week. In January however, always and without fail, we'd have the Seville orange show. I'm not marmalade's biggest fan, so when the researcher asked, 'Lotte, any original ideas for marmalade?'. I replied, 'Hate the stuff, why don't we shove it up a chicken's bottom!'. And so Roast chicken with marmalade butter was born.

Serves 4

50g/2oz butter, softened
2 tablespoons Seville orange
   marmalade
1 piece preserved stem ginger in syrup,
   drained and chopped
2kg/4$\frac{1}{2}$lb free-range chicken
1 small onion
salt and freshly ground black pepper
roast potatoes and steamed purple
   sprouting broccoli or curly kale, to
   serve

Preheat the oven to 180°C/fan oven 160°C/gas mark 4.
Aga 4/3-door *Middle of baking oven.*
Aga 2-door *Grid shelf on floor of roasting oven with cold plain shelf on second set runners.*

Mix the butter, marmalade and stem ginger together. Season the inside of the chicken with salt and pepper and place the onion inside the cavity.

Gently tease the skin on the chicken breast away from the flesh. Place half the butter under the skin. Press down and spread it all around the breast area.

Spread the remaining butter all over the outside of the chicken.

Place a sheet of foil, approximately 75–100cm/2$\frac{1}{2}$ft–1yd long and large enough to make a loose tent over the chicken, in a roasting tin. Place the chicken on the foil and cover it loosely with the foil to form a tent. Secure the edges of the foil by folding them over.

Roast the chicken for 1$\frac{1}{2}$ hours. During this cooking time pull back the foil a couple of times and baste the chicken with the marmalade butter, making sure you return the foil to a tent.

After 1$\frac{1}{2}$ hours remove the chicken from the oven and open the foil. Baste the chicken with the juices and butter and then roast it, uncovered, for another 30 minutes.

Remove the chicken from the oven and transfer it to a plate. Cover it with the foil again and leave it in a warm place to rest for 10–20 minutes before serving.

Serve the chicken with roast potatoes, purple sprouting broccoli or kale and the marmalade butter (see Lotte's tips).

Lotte's tips
I wouldn't try to make gravy with the sediment left over in the roasting tin. Normally I'd say go ahead, give it a good scrape and pour in some wine. However because of the sugar in the marmalade, scraping the pan would only lead to misery and bitter gravy?. The marmalade butter at the bottom of the pan that comes out during cooking is all you'll need to spoon over the chicken. Pour that out of the tin and keep it warm and serve with the chicken.

february

Almost spring.
Got to get through Valentine's day
(the millions of cards I regularly
receive) and, every four years, a
marriage proposal, then the days will
be longer and hopefully the wind
coming from the south…

February can be so exhausting
(just ask my postman, John)!
So, I suggest you eat… a lot.

auntie mary's favourite chicken liver pate

Auntie Mary has a quite thing for my chicken liver pâté. I have, at times found her rifling through my freezer for a forgotten pot of it. As long as she gets a delivery of it every so often, she is happy, and nowadays doesn't tend to break into my house as regularly. Such is her love of this recipe. (For the sake of Auntie Mary's reputation as a wonderful, honest and lovely lady, I would like to say that the above is all made up – except for the bit where I say she has a thing for the pâté!) I like to serve this pâté with one of my instant chutneys (see below). I think warm chutney and cold pâté go so well with each other and are delicious served on toast or on small chunks of bread as canapés.

Serves 4

225g/8oz butter, softened
1 large onion, sliced
6 garlic cloves, crushed
450g/1lb chicken livers
110g/4oz unsmoked streaky bacon,
  roughly chopped
150ml/5fl oz red wine
1 sprig of fresh rosemary
1 fresh bay leaf
3 tablespoons brandy
salt and freshly ground black pepper
fresh rosemary and bay leaves, to
  garnish
toasted bread and Warm apple and date
  chutney (see opposite), to serve

Melt 50g/2oz of the butter in a large, non-stick frying pan. Add the onion

and half the garlic and cook gently for 10 minutes.

Add the chicken livers and bacon to the pan and fry them for 5 minutes.

Now add the red wine, herbs and rest of the garlic. Make sure you tuck the herbs under the livers so you really flavour the pâté. Bring up to the boil, cover and cook gently for 20 minutes or until the livers are cooked – they should be brown all the way through.

Remove the pan from the heat and allow the mixture to cool until lukewarm – if the pâté is too hot when you add the butter, it will split.

Remove the herbs from the cooled pâté and whizz it in a food processor until it is smooth. Alternatively you can press the mixture through a metal sieve – but this takes a little longer.

Beat in the remaining butter either in the food processor or by hand. Stir in the brandy and season to taste. Spoon the pâté into a serving dish and decorate with the bay and rosemary. Chill for an hour in the fridge before serving.

Serve the pâté on toast with some Warm apple and date chutney.

Lotte's tips

If you are not eating the pâté straight away, it is a good idea to seal it with a layer of melted, clarified butter – about 1cm/$\frac{1}{2}$ inch deep. To make clarified butter, very slowly melt 225g/8oz unsalted butter. The fats and solids in the butter will sink to the bottom of the pan and the clear clarified butter comes to the top – pour this over the pâté and leave it to set in the fridge. The butter topped pâté can be kept in the fridge for up to 5 days. Alternatively freeze it for up to 3 months.

Warm apple and date chutney

This isn't the sort of chutney that you have to keep for 6 weeks before you can eat it. It's instant chutney. It doesn't have the same proportion of vinegar and sugar that normal chutney has (which are the main preserving ingredients) and therefore it will only really last for about 10 days in the fridge. I can guarantee you'll eat it before that though! I love the versatility of my instant chutney and all the different ingredients you can add at different times of the year. Because you literally make it and then eat it, it means you can always rustle one up for unexpected guests. I adore it with cheese, leftover cold meat and of course Auntie Mary's favourite chicken liver pâté.

Serves 4

50g/2oz butter
1 large onion, chopped
1 large cooking apple, peeled and
    chopped
1 large eating apple, peeled and
    chopped
50g/2oz fresh or dried dates, chopped
balsamic vinegar, to taste
dark brown sugar, to taste
salt and freshly ground black pepper

Melt the butter in a medium saucepan, add the onion and cook it gently for 5 minutes.

Add the apples and dates to the pan, cover and cook for a further 10 minutes over a gentle heat.

Add the balsamic vinegar and sugar to taste, the chutney needs to have an equal sweet and sour flavour. Try adding 1 tablespoon of vinegar to 1 dessertspoon of sugar to start with and continue until you get a flavour you're happy with

Season to taste and serve warm.

If you are not using the chutney straight away, transfer it to a lidded plastic container and store in the fridge for up to 10 days. Heat through gently before serving.

smoked salmon kedgeree

I just love the flavour cooked smoked salmon brings to a dish. In fact if I'm completely honest I only really like smoked salmon when it's hot, I prefer the texture. And what's wonderful about this recipe is the fact that you don't have to faff around cooking the fish first – toss it all in together, give it a stir and... enjoy!

Serves 4–6

225g/8oz basmati rice
50g/2oz butter
1 medium onion, finely chopped
1 small leek, finely sliced
2 teaspoons ground coriander
2 teaspoons ground cumin
2 teaspoons ground turmeric
$\frac{1}{2}$ teaspoon chilli powder
275g/10oz smoked salmon, cut into
    strips
4 tablespoons double cream
2 heaped tablespoons chopped fresh
    parsley
grated zest and juice of 1 lemon
4 hard-boiled eggs, quartered (see
    Lotte's tips)
salt and freshly ground black pepper
lemon wedges and chopped fresh
    parsley, to garnish

Cook the basmati rice according to the packet instructions. Rinse the cooked rice with boiling water and cool.

Melt the butter in a large, non-stick frying pan or wok and add the onion and leek. Cook gently for 5 minutes, stirring occasionally and then add all the dry spices and cook gently for 1–2 minutes.

Add the rice and stir for 1–2 minutes so the rice takes up the colour and flavour of the spices.

Toss the salmon into the pan and stir in the cream. Next add the parsley and lemon zest and juice. Season with a little salt and pepper and spoon into a serving dish.

Scatter over the cooked egg and garnish with the lemon wedges and chopped parsley.

Lotte's tips
To make perfect hard-boiled eggs: Bring a pan of salted water to the boil and add a drop or two of vinegar. Gently place the eggs into the water one by one and as you do, stir them around the pan in a circle – making a gentle whirlpool. When they are all in, stir again a few more times. This will ensure that the yolk sets perfectly in the centre of the egg white. Boil for 12 minutes.

When the 12 minutes is up, pour the water down the sink and then turn the cold tap on and keep it running over the eggs until they are completely cold. If you are water metered, probably best to put a plug in and fill the sink and let the eggs float in that! This will ensure that the nasty grey sulphur ring doesn't appear around the yolk – and the yolks will be lovely and yellow.

So, when you finally peel your egg and quarter it, the yolk will be sunny and centred – perfect.

peanut butter and raspberry jam biscuits

I can remember the first time I ate a peanut butter and jam sarnie. It was with my friend Laura. She was American and in my eyes, totally exotic. She taught me to say 'Hi' instead of boring 'Hello'. She was just so cool. Her father was working temporarily in Britain and had moved his family over here and they were our neighbours. When they came back from their visits to the States, they would bring back wonderfully exciting things like grape jelly! I'm sure I ate Pringles before anyone else did in this country. I sandwiched them with a gherkin – still do. We had Wotsits, they had Cheetos, we had sausages, and they had huge hot dogs, covered in mild yellow mustard within soft doughy bread. I loved her Lucky Charms cereal, her Lifesavers, Marshmallow Fluff and Hostess Twinkies. And then one day I discovered Reese's Peanut Butter Cups. Oh! They left me speechless as I let the chocolate melt in my mouth, only to discover the warm, slightly crunchy peanut butter hiding inside. It was all just too exciting! They called biscuits, cookies and jelly, Jell-O, then confused me by calling jam – jelly. And don't even get me started on the muffin debate!

Makes 6 large or 12 small biscuits

butter, for greasing
50g/2oz butter, softened
50g/2oz soft brown sugar
1 egg yolk
75g/3oz self-raising flour
$\frac{1}{2}$ tablespoon semi-skimmed milk
1 heaped tablespoon crunchy peanut butter
1 tablespoon raspberry jam

Preheat the oven to 180°C/fan oven 160°C/gas mark 4.
Aga 4/3-door *Middle baking oven.*
Aga 2-door *Grid shelf on floor roasting oven with cold plain shelf on second runners.*

Grease two baking sheets or line them with non-stick liner.

Cream the butter and sugar together until pale and fluffy. Add the egg yolk and beat well. Now stir in the flour, the milk and then the peanut butter. Finally stir in the jam, not completely, just enough to give it a ripple effect.

Divide the mixture into 6 or 12 and then roll into balls. Place the balls onto the baking sheets and flatten them down with a damp fork. Space the balls fairly well apart.

Bake for 10 minutes, checking on them halfway through, they should be golden brown. **Aga** *half way through, turn the baking sheet.*

Once cooked, leave on the sheet for 5 minutes then transfer to a wire rack to cool.

Lotte's tips
I use this basic mixture – butter, sugar, egg and flour – a lot. I like to serve biccies with coffee at my One to one cooking days and have come up with many variations in the past. You can add the zest of $\frac{1}{2}$ lemon, lime or orange. Or use just 50g/2oz of the flour and add 25g/1oz of ground almonds with a drop or two of almond extract. Any dried fruits are also lovely in these biscuits as are the occasional Smartie!

These yummy biscuits will keep for up to 3 days in an airtight container... if they last that long! Or they can be made ahead and frozen so you always have a supply to hand.

cauliflower soup with melted stilton and caramelised onions

I fear you may take a bit of convincing on this one. Cauliflower soup probably isn't on your 'Top ten meals to eat before I die' list. I can understand that. But I want you to trust me though – Cauliflower soup with luscious melted Stilton and sweet caramelised onions *is* the new black.

Serves 6–8

For the soup
25g/1oz butter
1 tablespoon olive oil
4 garlic cloves, crushed
1 large onion, sliced
2 bay leaves
a large sprig of fresh thyme
700g/1½lb potatoes, sliced
1 medium cauliflower, broken in to medium florets
850ml/1½ pints chicken stock
570–700ml/1–1¼ pints semi-skimmed milk
a pinch of freshly grated nutmeg
150g/5oz Stilton cheese, crumbled
salt and freshly ground black pepper

For the caramelised onions
2 tablespoons olive oil
2 onions, sliced
rye sour dough bread or crusty white bread, to serve

To make the soup, melt the butter and oil in a large saucepan and add the garlic and onion and cook gently for 10 minutes until soft. Don't let them brown though.

Add the bay leaves, thyme sprig, potatoes and cauliflower. Stir together.

Pour in the chicken stock and bring to the boil, partially cover the pan with a lid. Simmer the soup for 30 minutes or until the vegetables are tender. Remove the herbs.

Meanwhile to make the caramelised the onions, heat the oil in a medium, non-stick frying pan over a gentle heat and add the onions. Stir well so the onions are coated in the oil and leave to cook very gently for about 15–20 minutes or until they are a deep golden brown, stirring occasionally. If you gently cook the onion like this, it sweetens and mellows their flavour. Do make sure you keep the heat at a low-medium temperature otherwise they may burn. This makes them bitter and you'll have to start again!

Blend the soup until it is smooth, either using a hand held blender in the pan, or in a food processor and then return it to the pan. It will be quite a thick purée at this stage. Add 570ml/1pint of the milk and the nutmeg. Season with a little salt (you don't need much as the Stilton is quite salty) and pepper. If it still seems a bit too thick, add the remaining milk.

Stir in the Stilton cheese thoroughly, so it just starts to melt. Ladle the soup into bowls and top with some of the caramelised onions and serve with the bread.

Lotte's tips
There is enough here to serve 8 people because I wanted to give you a recipe that included a whole cauliflower, so you didn't have any waste. However, it freezes beautifully, without the Stilton or onions, so you can always store some in your freezer for another time. When defrosting, it will look like it has slightly separated, but don't panic because as you bring it up to the boil and stir it, it will come together nicely. Simply add some Stilton and onions once the soup has been thoroughly reheated.

mum's macaroni cheese

My mum was a fabulous cook, a natural. Hers was comfort food at its very best – full of heart and soul. She taught me all the basics of cooking and let me run riot in her kitchen. I used to try all the recipes from her 1950's Good Housekeeping book. I still have it now, and it's still one of my favourites. I miss my mum and I really miss her food. It's strange, but there are some dishes she used to cook that I've since tried, and as much I try to replicate the flavour, I can't. Her cauliflower cheese was historic and my hand always stretched towards that on the Sunday table, long before the roast chicken. It's odd to think I'll never taste her version of a recipe again. Never experience that familiarity. When she went, so did her experience and her funny ways with food. Here is her macaroni cheese, I've done my best to get it right and I hope she approves – cue bolt of lightning from above!

Serves 4

225g/8oz macaroni
40g/1½oz butter
4 tablespoons plain flour
570ml/1 pint semi-skimmed milk
a pinch of freshly grated nutmeg
1 tablespoon wholegrain mustard
1 teaspoon English mustard
1 tablespoon Worcestershire sauce
200g/7oz mature Cheddar cheese, grated
50g/2oz Gruyère cheese, grated
salt and freshly ground black pepper
4 tomatoes, sliced, to garnish
crusty bread and green salad, to serve

Preheat the oven to 200°C/fan oven 180°C/gas mark 6. **Aga 4/3/2-door** *Grid shelf on the floor of the roasting oven.*

Cook the macaroni according to the packet instructions and then drain it well.

Melt the butter in a medium, non-stick saucepan, remove from the heat and stir in the flour, mixing well. Now gradually add the milk, stirring all the time until it is completely incorporated. If it's a bit lumpy, get a whisk to it!

Return the pan to the heat and bring the sauce to the boil for 1 minute over a medium heat, stirring continuously with a wooden spoon, until it thickens.

Remove the pan from the heat again and stir in the nutmeg, mustards, Worcestershire sauce and seasoning. Go easy on the salt though as there is plenty in the cheese. Stir the cheeses into the sauce, reserving 1 tablespoon of the Cheddar.

Stir the cooked macaroni into the sauce to coat it thoroughly. Spoon the macaroni cheese into a 1.2 litre/2 pint ovenproof dish. Place the sliced tomatoes on top and sprinkle on a flourish of crispy bacon along with the reserved Cheddar cheese. Bake in the oven for about 20 minutes until golden and bubbling.

Serve with crusty bread and a green salad.

jamakewell tart

This used to be a Bakewell tart until my friend Jacqueline and I attacked it with rum, raisins and orange. We soaked the raisins overnight in rum and orange to give them a deliciously boozy flavour, gave the tart a quick name change and claimed it as ours. It was indeed a triumph, but hands off, we thought of it first! One Christmas, Jacqueline's husband, Graham, offered a One to one day cookery lesson with me as a present. If she liked it, Jacqueline could then have one a month for the whole year. Three years on and many, many days spent together in my kitchen cooking and chatting, Jacqueline has become one of my loveliest friends and still comes every month for a cookery day. She really doesn't need to, and is a fabulous cook, but the days are great fun and Jacqueline doesn't want to give them up! The soured cream and butter in this pastry make it all flaky and light. I think this pastry is superior to puff and without all the traditional folding and layering that takes so much time to do. Processing the butter and soured cream together, but not necessarily mixing it in thoroughly, contributes to this fabulous texture. During baking, the lumps of butter and soured cream melt within the dough and leave little gaps of air and this is what results in the light, buttery pastry, which although full of delicious cream and butter, isn't heavy or doughy. It's an absolute delight and my favourite pastry in the whole...wide...world!

Makes one 23cm/9 inch tart

For the shredded orange topping
1 orange
1 egg white
caster sugar
orange edible glitter

For the filling
110g/4oz raisins
2 tablespoons dark rum
grated zest and juice of 1 orange
110g/4oz butter, softened
110g/4oz light brown muscovado sugar
2 large eggs, beaten
175g/6oz amaretti biscuits, crushed
175g/6oz ground almonds

For the pastry
175g/6oz plain flour
150g/5oz unsalted butter, cubed and chilled
7 tablespoons soured cream
flour, for dusting
cream, ice cream or crème fraîche, to serve

Preheat the oven to 200°C/fan oven 180°c/gas mark 6. **Aga 4/3/2-door** *Grid shelf floor of roasting oven.*

The shredded orange topping needs to be made a day in advance. Using a potato peeler, peel off the orange zest in strips. Try not to go too deep and remove the white pith as you don't want that. Now even off the ends with a knife to make a rectangle out of each strip of zest and then slice them very thinly.

Blanch the strips for about 30 seconds in some boiling water and then strain through a sieve. Dry the strips on some kitchen paper.

Lightly whisk the egg white until it is frothy. Fill a saucer with some caster sugar. Dip each orange shred into the egg white, wipe off the excess and then toss in the sugar. Place each strip on some greaseproof paper. Repeat until you have done all the strips.

Leave the strips to dry overnight, uncovered, somewhere warm and then sprinkle with some edible glitter.

For the filling, place the raisins in a small bowl with the rum and orange juice and set aside to soak, overnight.

To make the pastry, place the flour in a food processor with the chilled and cubed butter. Whizz the flour and butter together until it resembles breadcrumbs. Add the soured cream and whizz again until the pastry just starts to come together. Turn the mixture out onto a floured worksurface and gently knead it together until a dough is formed. Wrap the pastry in clingfilm and chill for 1 hour.

Roll out the pastry on a floured worksurface and use it to line a deep 23cm/9-inch loose-based flan tin. Prick the pastry base with a fork. Drain the raisins and spoon them over the pastry. Reserve the rum and orange juice for later.

Cream the butter, sugar and orange zest together in a medium mixing bowl, using a wooden spoon, until pale and fluffy. Gradually add the beaten eggs, stirring well between each addition.

Mix the amaretti biscuits and the ground almonds together in a medium bowl and fold them into the mixture. Now fold in the reserved rum and orange juice.

Place the pastry case onto a large baking sheet. Spoon the filling into the case and smooth the top over using the back of a metal spoon.

Bake the tart for 15 minutes or until it begins to brown. Then reduce the temperature to 160°C/fan oven 140°C/gas mark 3 and cook for a further 10–20 minutes or until the filling is firm to the touch. **Aga 4/3-door** *Grid shelf on the floor of the baking oven.* **Aga 2-door** *Grid shelf on floor of roasting oven with cold plain shelf on third runners.*

Remove the tart from the oven and allow it to cool for 15 minutes, then you can remove it from the loose-based flan tin. Place a pudding basin upside down onto a worksurface and then gently place the tart on top. You'll find gravity does the rest as the sides of the tin will fall away from the edges of the pastry. Don't bother trying to remove the metal base, just serve the tart with it underneath – it's not really worth the worry of the tart possibly falling apart as you try and peel it off!

Sprinkle the orange shreds over the tart to decorate and add some more glitter if you like. Serve the tart warm, but not hot and indulge it with an enormous amount of cream, ice cream or crème fraîche.

salmon fish fingers and green sauce

I've never tried to mess with a cod fishfinger. I've heard they're mean and can break your arm with one swipe. Or is that a swan? Whatever...! Salmon on the whole are a lot kinder and make delicious fingers, especially when dipped in this fresh, herby mayonnaise. I like to coat them in coarse breadcrumbs (see tip, opposite) as I think they are nicer with a chunky crumb. These also make a great starter. You can also serve them as nibbles at drinks parties.

Serves 4

For the fishfingers
450g/1lb salmon fillet, skinned
75g/3oz plain flour
1/2 teaspoon salt
2 eggs, beaten
275g/10oz coarse fresh white
  breadcrumbs
8 tablespoons rapeseed oil
freshly ground black pepper
sea salt, for sprinkling

For the green sauce
8 tablespoons mayonnaise
2 tablespoons semi-skimmed milk
1 tablespoon chopped fresh chives
1 tablespoon chopped fresh parsley
1 tablespoon chopped fresh basil
2 spring onions, finely chopped
1/2 garlic clove, crushed
mushy peas and chips, to serve

Preheat the oven to 200°C/fan oven 180°C/gas mark 6.
Aga 4/3/2-door *Grid shelf on floor of roasting oven.*

Slice the salmon into eight fingers.

Mix the flour with the salt and some pepper. Place the seasoned flour, beaten eggs and breadcrumbs into three shallow bowls.

Toss the salmon fingers in the flour, shake off any excess and then dip them in the egg. Finally, place them in the breadcrumbs and make sure they are well covered with no salmon showing through.

Place the coated salmon in the fridge, to chill and firm up, for at least an hour before you cook them.

In the meantime make the Green sauce. Spoon the mayonnaise into a small serving bowl and add the milk. Stir well to make a sauce with a good pouring/dipping consistency. Add the herbs, spring onion and garlic and mix well.

Heat the oil in a large, non-stick, heavy-based frying pan and fry the salmon fingers for about 5–6 minutes on either side. Make sure they are cooked through – the flesh will go from being a raw darker pink to a light pink with a flaky texture. You can also test to see if they are cooked by slipping a sharp knife gently into the middle of a fishfinger, leaving it there for 10 seconds and then removing it. Carefully test the

temperature of the knife – if it is only lukewarm, the fishfingers need longer cooking.

Drain on some kitchen paper and then sprinkle with some sea salt. Serve with a good dollop of the sauce and perhaps some mushy peas and chips!

Making your own breadcrumbs
If you have any bread that is a little stale, or any crusts to spare, give them a whizz in the food processor (not too long or they'll be too fine), bag and freeze. Then, you've always got them to hand for rissoles, fishcakes, bread pudding or thickening sauces and stews.

 March

It's so nearly spring now.
In March I feel the first stirrings
of seed packet frenzy. This can
start in any garden centre.
I'm really not that fussy.

I can spend hours head-deep
in the seed section at Burford Garden
Centre, only coming up for air
when I've got at least four different
types of sweet pea, three carrots,
stripy beetroot and some
yellow courgettes!

Sometimes, I meet with my lovely friend, Jennie, at Burford Garden Centre. After an age spent with me trawling for seeds, we become a little parched. My blood sugar's on the floor and Jennie has quite rightly lost patience. So we embark on another frenzy – one that involves lots of cake. We make haste to their restaurant!

We first met over tea and chocolate cake 21 years ago. We'd both just had babies. Our health visitor told each of us that there was another nice young girl who'd just had a baby in the lane, and wouldn't it be lovely if you were friends. Those few lines are usually the death knell to any friendship, but I thought I'd take a chance and knock on her door one afternoon.

That was at midday. At six o'clock we were still chatting, eating cake and drinking tea. Oliver and Daisy spent the first six years of their life completely inseparable. They adored each other then and are still the closest of chums.

Jennie and I met with cake and we still do cake an awful lot!

Cake is a marvellous thing. It makes you happy. If people ate more of it, the world would be a better place. I'm sure there would be fewer wars in the world, if peace could be discussed over a nice slice of Victoria sandwich.

Politicians who have mouths full of crumbly cake, buttery icing and raspberry jam might not feel the need to blow up another country. Oh, I can see them now; embracing each other lovingly whilst offering around coffee and walnut cake or squidgy lemon slices. Cherry cake, filled with lashings of cream, dark red cherries and sour cherry jam would be all they'd need to fulfil their nuclear ambitions. Who needs a missile when you can have a fairy cake? Who wants to invade a nation when you can close your eyes and enjoy the bliss that is a squidgy chocolate cake?

You see? Cake. World peace sorted.

Politicians who have mouths full of crumbly cake, buttery icing and raspberry jam might not feel the need to blow up another country.

steamed cherry bakewell pudding with sherry sauce

I woke up one Sunday morning, having indulged myself enormously the night before. Not a good day to be cooking lunch for eight. Head sitting in my hand at a jaunty angle and shuffling around in my slippers, I managed to (somewhat haphazardly) bung the meat in the oven to roast and prepare the vegetables. Next, during my much longed for hot shower, I suddenly remembered pudding. In the panic I catapulted myself across the landing, caught my hip on the door, swore and shook my fist at the wretched door, kicked it and then regretted it, threw some clothes on and vaulted down the stairs. Hopping and limping – and still a little soggy, I tried to find some inspiration. Not easy when you would rather someone just come and put you out of your misery. But then I thought steamed pudding, nice and easy to cook – and forget! A steamed pud doesn't mind hanging around for a while – it's quite a patient little fellow. What's in the cupboard? Half a jar of cherry jam, the usual suspects and some ground almonds. Eureka! Muddle together, pour into the greased pudding basin and steam for 1½ hours. Genius! The original Bakewell pudding was the result of a mistake. This one came from a hangover... enjoy!

Serves 4

For the pudding
butter, for greasing
110g/4oz butter, softened
110g/4oz soft brown sugar
2 eggs, beaten
a few drops of almond extract
75g/3oz self-raising flour, sieved
75g/3oz ground almonds
2 tablespoons semi-skimmed milk
3 tablespoons cherry jam

For the sherry sauce
25g/1oz butter
25g/1oz plain flour
275ml/10fl oz semi-skimmed milk
1 heaped tablespoon caster sugar
1 tablespoon double cream
2 tablespoons medium sherry

Butter a 900ml/1½ pint pudding basin.

Cream the butter and sugar together in a medium mixing bowl, using a wooden spoon or electric whisk, until pale and fluffy. Add the eggs, beating well after each addition.

Stir in the almond essence and then fold in the flour and almonds. Add the milk to give a dropping consistency.

Spoon the jam into the bottom of the pudding basin and then pour the pudding mixture on top.

Cover the bowl with a large piece of greased greaseproof paper or foil and secure it in place with string.

Half fill a steamer or large saucepan with boiling water and steam the pudding for 1½ hours. Make sure you keep an eye on the water level and top it up with boiling water at intervals if necessary.

Aga 4/3/2-door *Bring to the boil and steam the pudding on the simmering plate for 30 minutes, then transfer to the simmering oven for 1 hour. The simmering oven is very kind though, so if you need to leave if for bit longer, it should be fine.*

About 15 minutes before the pudding has finished cooking, make the Sherry sauce, melt the butter in a small non-stick saucepan, stir in the flour and cook for 1–2 minutes, stirring all the time with a wooden spoon to make a roux. Now remove from the heat and gradually add the milk, stirring all the time, until it is completely incorporated. Beat well.

Return the pan to the heat and bring to the boil, stirring all the time. Simmer gently for a couple of minutes and then add the sugar. Stir in the cream and sherry. If you want to add a little more sugar to taste, then go ahead.

Turn the pudding out of the basin and serve it with the warm Sherry sauce.

Lotte's Tips
I often serve this Sherry sauce, as my mother did every year, with Christmas pudding. (page 186)

three colour medieval soup

Imagine a bowl with three different colours of soup in it. A medieval idea and a bonkers one. But everyone was a bit bonkers then – men wore tights, funny shoes and knocked each other off horses for fun. Seriously though, a bit of history now... in medieval times, colour was very important in food. Many dishes were made with bright, colourful sauces. They used saffron for yellow, sandalwood for red, and for green they added parsley and spinach. So, one third of this soup is red, but I use tomato instead of sandalwood, which quite honestly I think would be hideous and probably not very digestible! Tomatoes didn't come to our shores until Elizabethan times and actually, neither did potatoes – they would have used bread or parsnips to thicken the soup. So tomatoes are not medieval in the slightest, well not in Britain anyway, and they weren't eaten properly until the 19th century – the reason being that they were thought of as aphrodisiacs, hence the original name the love apple! But I am going to ignore this and add them to this soup anyway as I just love the colour combination and flavour. For the yellow and green parts of the soup I stick with tradition and use saffron and spinach to add vibrant colour and subtle flavour.

Serves 4

50g/2oz butter
1 large onion, sliced
3 garlic cloves, crushed
700g/1½lb potatoes, evenly diced
  (I like to use King Edwards)
150ml/5fl oz dry white wine
1 litre/1¾ pints vegetable stock
1 fresh bay leaf, split (this releases its
  natural oil and intensifies the
  flavour)
a pinch of saffron strands
175g/6oz frozen spinach, thawed
150ml/5fl oz double cream
2 heaped tablespoons tomato purée
150ml/5fl oz tomato juice
1 tablespoon chopped fresh parsley
salt and freshly ground black pepper
1 tablespoon chopped fresh chives, to
  garnish
Leek and cheese soda bread (see 48),
  to serve

Melt the butter in a large saucepan and add the onion. Cook it over a gentle heat for 10 minutes.

Add the garlic and the potatoes and cook for another 5 minutes. Add the wine and simmer for a couple of minutes. Now pour in the stock, add the bay leaf, bring up to the boil and simmer for 30 minutes with the lid half on.

Place the saffron strands in a cup and pour over 1 tablespoon of boiling water. Set aside. Place the thawed frozen spinach in a sieve and press out the excess moisture with the back of a spoon. Leave the spinach in the sieve until you are ready to use it.

When the soup is cooked, either using a hand held blender in the pan, or in a food processor blend it until it is smooth and then return it to the pan. Add the cream and season with salt and pepper. Take two-thirds of the soup out of the pan and divide it equally between two saucepans. Add the tomato purée and juice to the original pan, the saffron and water to the other and the spinach and parsley to the final saucepan. Heat the soups through until they are piping hot. Taste each soup and adjust the seasoning if necessary.

Put one ladle of each colour soup into a bowl, trying not to let the colours mix too much. Sprinkle each bowl with a few of the chopped chives and serve with delicious Leek and cheese soda bread.

Lotte's tips
Now, I know I mentioned at the beginning of the book my loathing for recipes that require many saucepans – but please forgive me for this one and only small misdemeanour in the above recipe – it's the only time I'll ask you to use three saucepans at once for one recipe in this book!

fish pie with the girls

I arranged a supper for some of the girls. We were 6 opinionated, strong birds all sat at my round table in my very old dining room. A recipe for democratic disaster you might think – but actually no. Not a knife was thrown, not a cross word expelled. We sorted the world, spoke about how much we adore men (as long as they do as they're told), nattered shoes and laughed until we wet our pants! This often happens after childbirth. Oh yes, and we drank a smidgen of wine. The dining room forms the original part of my cottage and is circa 1640. I can only imagine how many fantastic times have been had in there. It has a wonderful atmosphere and when lit by candles at night, is the prettiest and cosiest of rooms. Because I spend a large part of my life cooking and serving for a living, when I have friends to dinner, I'm fully aware I turn into a terrible hostess. I just want to relax and cook easy food that doesn't take too much effort during the evening. It all starts so well. Everyone arrives; we drink fizz in the kitchen and eat the starter there – usually, many substantial canapés. The main course is always a dish that I have prepared in advance and can bring out of the oven without any fuss. Hence the Fish pie. At this stage I am well on my way to being a little tipsy, so if someone else can carry it from the kitchen – even better. It's devoured and apparently cleared away – by now I'm sooo relaxed, I'm stuck to my chair. Good friends know at this point, that they have to hunt out the pudding themselves. It can usually be found in the fridge. This too has been prepared in advance, because I'm a clever, devious hostess and I know that by the pudding, I've basically lost interest in serving anyone. It's every man for himself with the coffee. I don't care. I don't drink it after three in the afternoon anyway.

Serves 6

For the topping
1.3kg/3lb potatoes, diced (I especially like Rooster potatoes)
75g/3oz butter
55ml/2floz hot semi-skimmed milk
salt and freshly ground black pepper

For the pie
butter, for greasing
50g/2oz butter
5 tablespoons plain flour
425ml/15fl oz semi-skimmed milk
150ml/5fl oz double cream
4 heaped tablespoons chopped fresh parsley
2 heaped tablespoons chopped fresh chives
225g/8oz pollock fillet, skinned and cut into bite-size chunks
225g/8oz salmon fillet, skinned and cut into bite-size chunks
110g/4oz smoked salmon, cut into strips
225g/8oz cooked and peeled prawns
225g/8oz streaky bacon, cut into strips
2 tablespoons chopped fresh parsley, to garnish
peas, to serve

Preheat the oven to 200°C/fan oven 180°C/gas mark 6.
Aga 4/3/2-door *Grid shelf on the floor of roasting oven.*

Butter a 1.7litre/3 pint ovenproof dish.

Place the potatoes in a large pan of salted water, bring to the boil and cook for 15–20 minutes or until tender. Drain and mash with the butter, hot milk and plenty of seasoning. Keep warm.

Melt the butter in a large, non-stick saucepan, stir in the flour and cook for 1–2 minutes, stirring all the time with a wooden spoon to make a roux. Remove from the heat and gradually add the milk, stirring all the time, until it is completely incorporated. Beat well and use a whisk if there are any lumps! Place back onto the heat and bring up to the boil, stirring all the time and simmer for 1–2 minutes. This sauce is quite thick, so don't worry. Once the fish is added and it cooks in the oven, it will thin out a bit and be the perfect consistency.

Stir the double cream, parsley, chives and seasoning into the sauce. Add the fish and prawns and carefully stir them in. Take the pan off the heat and pour the fish mixture into the greased ovenproof dish. Cover with the mashed potato and fluff up with a fork.

Bake the pie for 30–40 minutes, until it is heated all the way through and the potato is golden. While the pie is baking, fry the bacon strips in a large, non-stick frying pan until they are crisp and golden brown.

When the pie is cooked sprinkle over the strips of crispy bacon. Garnish with the parsley and serve with peas and plenty of wine.

march plum cake

I know, I know plums aren't in season in March, but when I came up with this cake, I had some kicking around, looking a bit dodgy, in the bottom of my fridge. Jennie was coming for tea along with some other friends, including the 2-year-old twins from next door. Whenever my name is mentioned to the twins, they say 'Lotte cake'; so under considerable pressure to perform and be the cake queen/mistress/doyenne of my lane, I used the shrivelled old fruit, crossed my fingers and March plum cake made its first entrance into the world. Tension was in the air as Olive and Alice picked up a slice of cake with their chubby little fingers. A small bead of nervous sweat appeared on my brow as I watched them closely for their reaction. All eyes fell on their befuddled expressions as they bit into the dense almondy cake and got squidgy plums down their best dresses. "No pressure girls, but... do... you... like... my... cake?" They didn't answer as, in a split second before any of us could react; they had buried their entire faces into the rest of the cake. I'll take that as a 'yes' then!

Makes one 23cm/9 inch cake

butter, for greasing
8 plums, halved and stoned
225g/8oz butter, softened
225g/8oz soft brown sugar
grated zest of ½ orange
4 large eggs
175g/6oz self-raising flour, sieved
½ teaspoon baking powder
50g/2oz ground almonds

Preheat the oven to 180°C/fan oven 160°C/gas mark 4. **Aga 4/3-door** *Middle of baking oven.* **Aga 2-door** *Grid shelf on floor of roasting oven with cold plain shelf on second runners.*

Grease and line a 23cm/9-inch springform cake tin.

Place the plum halves, skin side down, on the bottom of the prepared cake tin.

Cream the butter, sugar and orange zest together in a medium mixing bowl, using a wooden spoon or electric whisk, until pale and fluffy.

Beat the eggs into the creamed mixture, one at a time. Add 1 teaspoon of flour to the mixture between each addition. This is quite a runny cake mixture so don't worry. It might even look a bit curdled, but it's absolutely fine. The large eggs make for a lovely moist eggy cake that tastes delicious.

Using a metal spoon, fold in the rest of the flour, the baking powder and the ground almonds and pour the mixture over the plums in the cake tin.

Spread the mixture evenly in the tin with the back of a metal spoon and bake for 30 minutes. Then remove, cover loosely with foil and continue to cook for another 30 minutes.

Remove the cake from the oven and leave it to cool for 5 minutes in the tin and then turn it out onto a wire rack. I like to serve this warmish as it is lovely and squidgy.

leek and cheese soda bread

The quickest and yummiest of breads... and fab with the wonderfully cheering Three colour medieval soup (see page 42).

Makes one 23cm/9-inch round loaf

butter, for greasing
1 tablespoon rapeseed oil
1 large leek, thinly sliced
$^1/_2$ tablespoon dried sage
75g/3oz mature English Cheddar, grated
450g/1lb self-raising flour
1 teaspoon salt
1 large egg, beaten
275ml/10fl oz buttermilk
1–2 tablespoons semi-skimmed milk
flour, for dusting
freshly ground black pepper

Preheat the oven to 190°C/fan oven 170°C/gas mark 5.
Aga 4/3-door *Top of baking oven.*
Aga 2-door *Grid shelf on floor of roasting oven.*

Grease a baking sheet with butter.

Heat the oil in a medium, non-stick frying pan and add the leek and cook gently for about 10 minutes, until it is just starting to brown. Add the sage and allow to cool.

Put the leeks and sage in to a large mixing bowl with the cheese, flour, salt and some freshly ground black pepper. Add the beaten egg to the mixture. Now gradually add the buttermilk until you have a smooth dough. You might need to add the extra milk. Don't worry if the dough is sticky. Transfer the dough to a floured worksurface and knead it to bring it together. Form the dough into a round approximately 23cm/9 inches in diameter.

Pop the dough onto the greased baking sheet and press it down to form a round. Make deep cuts across the top to make 6 wedges and bake the bread in the oven for about 30–35 minutes until golden brown. Transfer to a wire rack to cool.

The bread is best served warm, but it will keep for a couple of days if it doesn't all disappear as soon as you serve it!

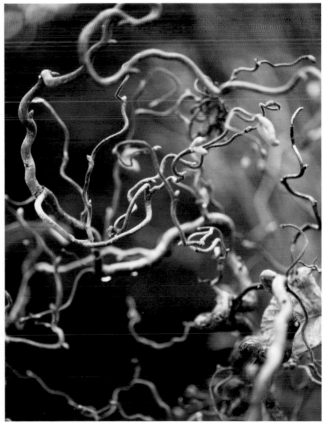

april

I try to resist a daffodil in
my house until April.

I try not to buy them; I like to pluck
them straight from my garden.
I loathe planting bulbs in autumn, but
the hard work and sprained wrists I
receive as I try to dig through clay are
worth it when April heralds the yellow
daffadowndilly of my childhood.
Easter was only Easter when they were
in the house, scenting the hallway.

I just adore these sunny, spring flowers.

I have two cats. Some say, two cats too many. And even though I love them both to bits, on occasion I agree. Honeybear and The Woozle are their names.

Honey is a mild mannered, (unless you try to inject or de-flea her) sweet, friendly, pudding-sized ginger cat – with big bones and a weight issue. We don't mention it too much in front of her, in case we offend. Offending Honey can lead to a territorial widdle in the fireplace.

The Woozle is feral six months of the year – during the summer she forgets where she actually lives, as her home is where she lays her tail. Unfortunately this is often just outside a rabbit warren. On the rare occasion she does bound in, like the prodigal cat with a spring in her step and haughty eyes, she brings home rabbit fleas and a stinking attitude. Many love her, my friend Amanda, for example. She requests photos of The Woozle all the time, but, alas, no sleight of hand nor speed of shutter could ever capture The Woozle.

The thing is, they don't have to live with her. I do. Please don't think I am a Woozle-hating cat person. I'm not; she does have some excellent qualities about her. I suppose she's always friendly, and does have a sweet squirrel tail thing going on. And of course in the winter, she fattens up and tries her best to look cute, all curled up in front of the fire. She doesn't cost much to feed in the summer (rabbit is cheap) and she's good entertainment – The Woozle can dance. If you click your fingers high and say 'Woozle dance' in a sing-songy, irritating kind of way she jumps onto her hind paws and does a pirouette. A very talented cat really.

Honeybear, on the other hand doesn't stray out of the garden. She's scared of pretty much everything, and has the appetite of a labrador which is why she is on the porky side.

Quick, she's gone downstairs. Have to be speedy – race you to my bowl. Come on then, pour it in, pour it in, pour it in … if I could just knock her hand with my head, I might get more..... Yes!

Munch, munch, munch. And … munch, munch, munch. And … munch. Any stray biscuits on the floor? Munch.

Honey is a mild mannered, (unless you try to inject or de-flea her) sweet, friendly, pudding-sized ginger cat – with big bones and a weight issue.

My perfect day, by Honeybear

"Wake up – possibly if I'm lucky on my fabulous owner's bed. Little yawn, a stretch with bum in the face of my fabulous owner. Ah, she's not awake yet – OK off to the creaky floorboard, for a bit of wobbling. I like surfing on a bit of elm (Hawaii Five O music in my ears).

Still not awake? Ugh. Right, time to pull out the trump card – if I can just balance myself on the bedside table and … leap – fabulous, she's awake! Can't understand why I've just been shouted at. Bit mean really.

Ok, bit of food, bit of food, bit of food. Now! Alright then, just a little tickle on my –Oh! Where's she gone?

Now, a little wander around my land, check everything is in order. Nice and steady now, just eaten don't want indigestion. Lovely, the herbaceous borders are looking good, lawn is neatly mowed. Couple of weeds, oh dear, fabulous owner is slacking.

That mouse looks a bit big and scary – might leave it for The Woozle. Now, need nice patch of clean earth for a quick... ah, lovely feel better. Cover it up. Little wander, nice sunny bit of grass. Pat down the grass underneath my favourite bush. And sleep. Must remember to wake up at three o'clock for food time. Snore."

Honey's uncanny can habit...

Another nutty and somewhat strange habit Honey has is to know exactly when I am opening a can of tuna. I have been jumped on, on so many occasions, that now whenever I open a can of tuna I have to sing opera very loudly. If Honey hears the turn of the opener, she knows it's going to be tuna. If she knows it's going to be tuna I have a fight on my hands, a battle of wills and a cat attached to my leg.

So, using stealth tactics the SAS would be proud of, I now have to sing a (rather good, if I say so myself) rendition of Ave Maria in time with each turn of the opener. If, for example I am stuffing a jacket potato with tuna, I have to proceed gently on tip-toes to the fridge where I remove the mayonnaise, cucumber, red pepper and celery. Sidle to the sink where I drain the tuna and sing Pia Jesu as I rinse out the can. I then pile the lot inside the potato and eat it sitting on top of the table, whilst Honey (who has heard me) slopes around like a stalking shark. I fear she may be developing a love of opera.

hot cross bun, chocolate and rum pudding

Let's think fluffy bunnies, chocolate eggs, baby chicks and Easter. If a pudding could draw a naughty line, this one would triple jump it!

Serves 6–8

butter, for greasing
6 hot cross buns, halved
5 tablespoons chocolate hazelnut
  spread
12 ready-to-eat pitted prunes, halved
275ml/10fl oz double cream
275ml/10fl oz semi-skimmed milk
150g/5oz 70% cocoa solids dark
  chocolate
4 eggs
1 tablespoon dark brown sugar
3 tablespoons dark rum
single cream, to serve

Preheat the oven to 180°C/fan oven 160°C fan oven/gas mark 4.
Aga 4/3-door *Middle of baking oven.*
Aga 2-door *Grid shelf on floor of roasting oven with cold plain shelf on second runners.*

Grease a 1.7 litre/3 pint ovenproof dish with the butter.

Spread each side of the hot cross buns with the hazelnut and chocolate spread and then place 4 prune halves inside each bun. Sandwich the buns back together and then cut each bun into four and place in the bottom of the ovenproof dish.

Heat the cream, milk and the chocolate together in a small non-stick saucepan over a gently heat, stirring all the time. Take care not to bring the mixture to the boil. Cool slightly.

Beat the eggs and sugar together in a large mixing bowl and add the rum. Pour the chocolate cream over the egg mixture and stir well.

Now pour the chocolate mixture over the buns and leave to soak for 30 minutes.

Bake for 30–40 minutes or until the pudding is firm in the middle. If it starts to catch on top, cover with a little foil.

Serve with single cream – heaven!

smoked salmon soup with blue cheese muffins

This soup is in fact leek and potato soup in disguise. It freezes well (see my tips), as do the quick and easy Blue cheese Muffins that I love to serve it with. It's a combination that adds up to one of my favourite lunchtime numbers.

Serves 4–6

50g/2oz butter
2 large leeks, sliced
2 large garlic cloves, crushed
700g/1½ lb, potatoes, chopped into medium chunks
150ml/5fl oz dry white wine
1 litre/1¾ pints vegetable stock
1 fresh bay leaf, split (this releases its natural oil and intensifies the flavour)
¼ teaspoon dried thyme
150ml/5fl oz double cream
225g/8oz smoked salmon, cut into strips
salt and freshly ground black pepper
2 tablespoons chopped fresh chives, to garnish
Blue cheese muffins, to serve

Melt the butter in a large saucepan and add the leeks, garlic and potatoes. Cook them gently, for about 10 minutes over a low heat, until the leeks are soft. Stir the vegetables a few times to prevent them from sticking.

Add the wine to the pan, bring it up to the boil and allow it to simmer for 2 minutes. Pour in the stock, add the herbs, bring to the boil and simmer with the lid half on for about 30 minutes.

Remove the bay leaf and whizz the soup in a blender until it is smooth, then return it to the pan. Reheat the soup and season with a pinch of salt and some black pepper (the salmon is quite salty so you won't need much extra salt). Stir in the cream.

To serve, divide the salmon between 4 or 6 warmed soup bowls. Ladle the soup into the bowls, sprinkle over the chopped chives and serve with the Blue Cheese Muffins below.

Lotte's tips

I freeze the soup without the salmon. Make sure the reheated soup is piping hot and then pour it over the smoked salmon in the bowls, as above, this is enough to heat the salmon through.

Blue cheese muffins

Blue cheese happens to be one of my favourites and pine nuts number one on my seed scale. The combination of both amid the soft and bouncy muffin sponge is far beyond any form of decency. I rarely manage to give any away. I resent bestowing them upon friends, neighbours and dinner guests (and they know better than to take one without asking). Simply, utterly and completely wonderful: a triumph when served with my Smoked Salmon Soup, but also a joy for breakfast, snacks, lunch, supper, midnight feast, picnic or barbecue. And if you don't like blue cheese? A strong Cheddar or perhaps goat's cheese will suffice. And if you don't like either of them? Eat toast.

Makes 6 large muffins

200g/7oz self-raising flour
150g/5oz soft blue cheese, crumbled
2 tablespoons chopped fresh chives
2 tablespoons chopped fresh parsley
1 tablespoon sunflower seeds
1 tablespoon pine nuts
½ teaspoon salt
120ml/4fl oz semi-skimmed milk
150ml/5fl oz sunflower oil
1 egg

Preheat the oven 180°C/fan oven 160°C/gas mark 4.
Aga 4/3-door *Middle of baking oven.*
Aga 2-door *Grid shelf on floor of roasting oven with cold plain shelf on second runners.*

Place 6 large paper muffin cases in a 6-hole large muffin tray,

In a large mixing bowl, mix the flour, blue cheese, herbs, sunflower seeds, pine nuts and salt together.

Combine the milk, sunflower oil and egg in a measuring jug. Make a well in the centre of the dry ingredients and pour in the wet mixture. Stir lightly until only just combined.

Spoon the mixture into the muffin cases, filling each one two-thirds full.

Bake the muffins for 20–25 minutes until they are firm and the tops are golden brown. Remove the muffins from the tray and place on a wire rack. Serve warm

daisy's banana cake

For years my daughter Daisy has informed me that her version of this totally delicious cake is the best. For many years I have considered this and tried my very best to make a better one. Unfortunately for my ego, I've failed and I can now declare in front of you all and to my intense irritation, that Daisy's is indeed the very best banana cake in the whole wide world if not the universe....and beyond.

Makes one 900g/2lb loaf

2 over-ripe bananas
juice of $\frac{1}{2}$ lemon
110g/4oz butter, softened
110g/4oz soft brown sugar
2 large eggs, beaten
225g/8oz self-raising flour, sieved
50g/2oz sultanas
1 piece preserved stem ginger in syrup, drained and finely chopped
$\frac{1}{2}$ teaspoon cinnamon
$\frac{1}{2}$ teaspoon ground ginger
$\frac{1}{2}$ teaspoon of baking powder
softened butter, to serve (optional)

Preheat the oven to 180°C/fan oven 160°C/gas mark 4. **Aga 4/3-door** *Middle of the baking oven.* **Aga 2-door** *Grid shelf on floor of roasting oven with cold plain shelf on second runners.*

Grease and line a 900g/2lb loaf tin with greaseproof paper.

Place the bananas and lemon juice in a medium mixing bowl, mash them together using a fork and set aside.

Cream the butter and sugar together in a medium mixing bowl, using a wooden spoon or electric whisk, until pale and fluffy. Add the eggs a little at a time, beating well after each addition. Add the mashed banana and beat well.

Now, using a metal spoon, gently fold in the flour, sultanas, ginger, spices and baking powder and turn the mixture into the loaf tin. Spread it out evenly and give the mixture a little tap to settle it down in the tin.

Bake for 35–45 minutes until golden brown and firm to the touch. If you test with a knife in the middle, it will come out a little wetter than a normal cake, so don't worry, that's just the banana. As long as the cake is firm and not wobbly, it's cooked.

Remove from the oven, leave to cool in the tin for 5 minutes and then turn out onto a wire rack.

Serve sliced and spread with some softened creamy butter for an indulgent tea-time treat.

Lotte's tips
This will keep fresh for up to 3 days, wrapped in foil and greaseproof paper, in an airtight container.

Wild garlic, sorrel and nettle tart with cheesy pastry

In April my small patch of wild garlic comes to life. The sorrel is up and doing its thing and the nettles are beginning their assault on my poor defenceless garden. In the spring, I start to look at nettles in a very different way. I gaze upon them with a slightly carnivorous eye – if you can do that with a nettle. My body is telling me to eat them. My body knows that nettles really help to spring clean it and give it a boost. Country folk have eaten nettles for hundreds and hundreds of years. They know what's good for them and so do I. Nettles are brimming with vitamins A and C and ... lots of other things with big words. It's a good idea to pick the leaves with gloves, and please don't try to eat them raw – they will sting! Don't pick them during or after flowering as the leaves can be an irritant – you need to eat the nettles before they have flowered. It's probably best not to pick them if they are by the road or have been sprayed by insecticide or... a cat! To use nettle leaves, first blanch them in boiling water, then refresh under cold running water. Then just stir them into sauces, pasta or rice. Or mix them with some delicious wild garlic and sorrel and put them in this absolutely scrumptious tart, which has the best and easiest pastry you'll ever make. You no longer need to gaze upon nettles with contempt – think of them as a potential super food. This tart is particularly good served with a lovely salad of early summer greens and herbs – try my English herb and flower salad (page 88) – it's a beautiful combination!

Makes one 23cm/9 inch tart

225g/8oz butter, finely cubed
225g/8oz self-raising flour
225g/8oz mature Cheddar cheese, grated
2 tablespoons chopped fresh chives
a large handful each of nettles, wild
 garlic leaves and sorrel (stalks
 removed) or 3 large handfuls of fresh
 spinach and 2 heaped teaspoons
 snipped fresh chives
6 eggs
275ml/10fl oz double cream
1 tablespoon wholegrain mustard
1 heaped teaspoon Dijon mustard
salt and freshly ground black pepper
English herb and flower salad (see
 page 88), to serve

Preheat the oven to 200°C/fan oven 180°C/gas mark 6. **Aga 4/3/2-door** *Grid shelf on floor of roasting oven.*

First, make the pastry, place the butter and flour in medium mixing bowl and rub them together. Add the cheese and chives and squeeze together.

This is not a pastry that you roll as it is very sticky. You literally push and squidge it into a 3cm/1½ inch deep, 25cm/10-inch fluted loose-based flan tin. It's fun, I promise! As you push it in, make sure it is evenly spread and comes right up the sides of the tin. Also make sure there are no holes in the base or sides. Chill in the freezer for 15 minutes.

In the meantime, prepare the leaves. With gloves, remove the nettle leaves from the stem and then blanch them in a pan of boiling water for 1 minute.

Drain and place the nettles under a cold running tap to refresh them. Squeeze the water out by hand. At this stage you don't need gloves as the sting is removed from nettles when they are cooked. If you are using spinach, blanch it as for the nettles. Shred the wild garlic leaves and sorrel. Chop the chives, if using.

Beat the eggs, cream, mustard and seasoning together in a large jug. Add the nettles, sorrel and wild garlic leaves or spinach and chives and stir well.

Place the flan tin with the chilled pastry in onto a baking sheet. Pour the filling mixture into the pastry case.

Cook the tart for 15 minutes. Then reduce the temperature to 180°C/fan oven 160°C/gas mark 4 and cook until the centre of the tart is set and the pastry golden brown – this should take another 20–30 minutes. **Aga 4/3-door** *Place into the middle of the baking oven for the remainder of cooking time.* **Aga 2-door** *Put the cold sheet on the second set of runners for another 10 minutes, then place in the simmering oven until set.*

Leave the tart to cool in the tin for 10 minutes, then you can remove it from the tin. Place a pudding basin upside down onto a worksurface and then gently place the tart on top. You'll find the sides of the tin will fall away from the edges of the pastry. Don't fret about removing the metal base, just serve the tart with it underneath – it's not really worth the worry of the tart possibly falling apart as you try and peel it off!

potted salmon with sorrel

Potting your food as a means of preservation has always been popular in Britain. In the days before fridges and freezers, we had a choice between a cold pantry or outside. Or if you were rich, you might have an ice house. Mere mortals like me though, would pot. Pot anything. Meat, fish and cheese were all potted and then covered in a layer of fat to keep the air out and preserve the food. Sorrel is one of my favourite herbs and grows madly in my garden. It's just outside my kitchen door and one of the first bits of green herb to come up after the winter. Its acid green in colour and has a sour lemony flavour. It's fabulous in a salad and delicious in a buttery sauce. Salmon is quite a rich fish, strong in flavour and the sorrel cuts through it beautifully. This recipe is a fabulous way to use up leftover salmon and it has a lovely, light, gentle and mellow flavour to it. I often serve it up as a nice and easy starter, but it's just as delicious spread on fresh bread for lunch or supper.

Serves 2 as a main meal or 4 as a starter

225g/8oz cooked, skinned salmon
75g/3oz butter, softened
25g/1oz fresh sorrel or spinach, central
    stalks removed and roughly chopped
1 tablespoon dry sherry
$\frac{1}{2}$ teaspoon ground nutmeg
grated zest and juice of $\frac{1}{2}$ lemon
225g/8oz unsalted butter
salt and freshly ground black pepper

Remove any bones from the salmon. Pound it in a medium mixing bowl with a wooden spoon until the salmon is smooth and then work in the butter.

Mix in the sorrel or spinach and then add the sherry. Add the nutmeg, lemon zest and juice, and season with salt and pepper to taste.

Divide the mixture equally among 4 small pots or ramekins. Flatten it firmly with the back of a teaspoon so no bits will poke out through the clarified butter. Alternatively, you can serve it from one larger serving dish if you prefer.

To make the clarified butter to seal the potted salmon, very slowly melt the unsalted butter in a small pan over a gentle heat. The fats and solids in the butter will sink to the bottom of the pan and the clear clarified butter will come to the top.

Pour some clarified butter over each pot or ramekin and cover each one with cling film. Leave the potted salmon to chill in the fridge for a few hours or for up to 2 days before serving.

To serve, remove the potted salmon from the fridge about 10 minutes before serving to bring it back up to room temperature.

stuffed jacket potatoes

This is the indigenous food of my childhood. I've been trying to think of a suitable analogy to describe the feeling I get when I eat one of these. And I've finally come up with it – I can remember that warm and cosy feeling of being wrapped up in bed with the sheets and blankets pulled tightly around me and tucked under the mattress. I couldn't move and I didn't want to. I was bundled and swaddled and it felt lovely. Unfortunately for me, I have a duvet now, so can only get this feeling if I eat enough stuffed potatoes. Shame! I've included recipes for my two favourite jacket fillings here – Mushroom and bacon or Smoked haddock, pepper and spring onion. Each quantity of filling is for 4 potatoes so take your pick... and revel in the ultimate comfort food.

Serves 4

For the potatoes
4 large baking potatoes
rapeseed oil, for brushing
salt and freshly ground black pepper
salad or baked beans, to serve

For the mushroom and bacon filling
50g/2oz butter
1 medium onion, finely chopped
6 button mushrooms, sliced
175g/6oz smoked streaky bacon, finely
  chopped
4 tablespoons semi-skimmed milk
1 tablespoon chopped fresh parsley
110g/4oz Double Gloucester cheese,
  grated

For the smoked haddock, pepper and spring onion filling
225g/8oz smoked haddock
275ml/10fl oz semi-skimmed milk
50g/2oz butter
5 spring onions, finely chopped
1 red pepper, finely diced
110g/4oz Cheddar cheese, grated

Preheat the oven to 190°C/fan oven 170°C/gas mark 5. **Aga 4/3-door** *Top of baking oven.* **Aga 2-door** *Grid shelf on floor of roasting oven.*

Prick the potatoes with a fork and brush with a little oil. Place on a baking sheet and cook in the oven for $1^{1}/_{2}$–$1^{3}/_{4}$ hours. Meanwhile make your chosen filling.

For the Mushroom and bacon stuffed potatoes: While the potatoes are cooking, melt half the butter in a medium, non-stick frying pan and fry the onion and mushrooms for a couple of minutes until soft. Remove from the pan and set aside. Now add the remaining butter to the pan and then fry the bacon until crisp.

Cut the cooked potatoes in half and scoop out the potato flesh into a medium mixing bowl. Mash the cooked potato flesh well and add the milk and seasoning. Stir the vegetables, bacon and parsley into the potato mixture.

For the Smoked haddock, pepper and spring onion stuffed potatoes: While the potatoes are cooking, place the haddock, skin side up in a shallow frying pan and pour the milk over the top. Bring to the boil, cover and then simmer for 10 minutes. Remove from the heat. Peel the skin away from the flesh with a knife and fork and discard it. Leave the fish to cool in the milk. Melt the butter in a small, non-stick frying pan and fry the spring onions and pepper until soft. Flake the cooled fish, reserving the milk.

Cut the cooked potatoes in half and scoop out the potato flesh into a medium mixing bowl. Mash the cooked potato flesh well and add enough of the reserved milk to make the mash nice and creamy. Season the potato and then stir in the vegetables and haddock.

To cook the stuffed potatoes: Spoon the potato mixture back into the potato halves, cover with foil and return them to the oven for 10 minutes to heat through. Preheat the grill to high. Top the potatoes with the grated cheese and grill until the cheese is golden and bubbling. **Aga 4/3/2-door** *Top of the roasting oven to grill.* Serve immediately with salad or baked beans.

Lotte's tips
All tucked up tightly in napkins, these potatoes are perfect fodder for a cold November night too – one with fireworks. You can eat them without a fork, leaving one hand free for hot soup or warm cider.

May

What a truly glorious month May is. The air is warming up, the leaves on the bushes and trees are still that lovely bright acid green, and all of my blue and purple herbaceous plants are doing their thing.

OK, better get this on the record. I am an herbaceous plant addict. I can't help myself. I walk past one in a garden centre and I buy it. I see one in a magazine and it becomes a mission to hunt it down. I have two extra flower beds in my garden because of my addiction. I'm well on my way to a third.

fairy cakes with fruit icing and sparkles

I have lots of fairies in my garden. You have to look very carefully, but they are there. Generally they are very well behaved, but on occasion and when I cook these cakes, they can be a little cheeky. I think it might be the sparkles, or perhaps the fruity icing that sets them off. Whatever it is, the fairies can get a little bad tempered if you don't leave one by the toadstool for them. You're quite safe really because apart from the odd magic spell, they won't do you any harm. Although, saying that, the extra hair I sprouted on my chin did seem to come from nowhere...

Makes 12 cakes

For the cakes
110g/4oz butter, softened
110g/4oz caster sugar
grated zest of 1 lemon
2 eggs, beaten
110g/4oz self-raising flour, sieved

For the icing
50g/2oz fresh or frozen raspberries, puréed and sieved
flesh of 1 large, ripe passion fruit, sieved
110–150g/4–5oz icing sugar, sieved
sprinkles, sweeties, rose petals and edible glitter, to decorate

Preheat the oven to 190°C/fan oven 170°C/gas mark 5.
Aga 4/3-door *Top of baking oven.*
Aga 2-door *Grid shelf on floor of roasting oven.*

Place 12 paper cake cases in a 12-hole patty tin.

Cream the butter, sugar and lemon zest together in a medium mixing bowl, using a wooden spoon or electric whisk, until pale and fluffy. Add the eggs a little at a time and beat well between each addition using a wooden spoon. Fold in the flour using a metal tablespoon. Then using a teaspoon, fill each paper case two-thirds full.

Bake the cakes for 10–12 minutes, until golden and firm to the touch. Transfer the cakes to a wire rack to cool.

Add enough icing sugar to each fruit purée to make a soft, yet slightly firm icing.

Using a teaspoon, ice the cooled cakes and then finish them off with sprinkles, sweeties, rose petals or edible glitter or all of them!

Lotte's tips
You can also use blackcurrants or blackberries for the fruity icing, but don't bother with strawberries – I found the purée a bit thick to use and the flavour wasn't really strong enough. I have also used orange, lemon and lime zest and juice in the icing and they give a wonderfully zingy flavour.

pink meringues with clotted cream and strawberries

I believe that all meringues should be pink. Bright candy pink, and sandwiched together with clotted cream and ripe English strawberries. There is something about a meringue, especially a pink one that turns normal women into rather scary sugar monsters. Gentlemen, I would like to open your eyes to this one area of girl life. If you were present at a pink meringue feast, we would hold back, not wanting to look gluttonous or out of control. But without you there, we turn into she-devils with lustful meringue intentions that would bring tears to your eyes. We bury our faces in the marshmallowy centres, smear the buttery yellow cream over our lips and tumble handfuls of berries into our mouths. However, we don't do this in front of you; we wish you to think we're well behaved, elegant and sophisticated ladies, not pink meringue munching beasts!

Makes about 12 meringues

2 large egg whites
110g/4oz caster sugar
a few drops of red food colouring
clotted cream and fresh strawberries,
   to serve
icing sugar and pink edible glitter, to
   decorate (optional)

Preheat the oven to 120°C/fan oven 110°C/gas mark $^1/_2$. **Aga 4/3/2-door** *Simmering oven.*

Line a baking sheet with baking parchment or a non-stick liner.

Place the egg whites in a medium mixing bowl and whisk them until they are very stiff (see Lotte's tips), not floppy or runny, but really stiff!

Whisk 2 teaspoons of the sugar in and whisk again until the egg whites are really stiff.

Now your meringue is stable enough to fold in the rest of the sugar and a few drops of the colouring, with a large metal spoon. Add enough colouring to make your meringues a candy pink – the colour fades a little once they are cooked so be brave with the colouring. Do this gently so you don't knock any air out – you've just spent a long time whisking it in!

Next use a piping bag, fitted with a plain nozzle, to pipe an even number of tablespoon-sized mounds of meringue, spaced well apart, on the baking sheet or you can simply use a tablespoon to plop some down.

Bake the meringues for about 2 hours. After $1^1/_2$ hours, gently pick each meringue up and turn it on its side, then return them to the oven. This will dry out your meringues nicely. Transfer the cooked meringues to a wire rack to cool completely.

No more than an hour before you are ready to serve the meringues, pair them up and sandwich them together with a spoonful of clotted cream and a couple of sliced strawberries. Dust with a little icing sugar or even some pink edible glitter and eat enthusiastically.

Lotte's tips
You can use a balloon whisk for making meringues, but life really is a little easier if you have an electric one, because the most important thing about making meringues is to initially whisk the egg whites until they are very stiff indeed before you add any sugar. This is where so many people fall down. They don't whisk enough to begin with. As soon as you add sugar to whisked egg white it loosens and loses some of its bulk, so you need to make sure they are really stiff before you do.

The meringues can be made well in advance as they will keep for 10–14 days in an airtight container, and they also freeze well.

potted cheese with hazelnuts and tarragon

Potting cheese was, and is, a great way to use up the little bits of various hard cheeses that may be hiding in the bottom of your fridge. This was the original reason – you mashed up the odd bits, spiced them, threw some sherry at them and added some butter then sealed the pot with more butter and served it as a completely new dish. Over the last century, instead of using up old cheese, it became popular to make potted cheese with fresh cheese too – traditionally Cheshire. I've used Cheshire in this recipe and added a couple of other, slightly less traditional flavours. The combination of tarragon and hazelnuts might sound a bit barmy, but they work very well together. This potted cheese is delicious on warm, freshly baked bread.

Serves 4

25g/1oz hazelnuts
275g/10oz Cheshire cheese, grated and
    at room temperature
75g/3oz butter, softened
2 tablespoons dry sherry
2 tablespoons single cream
grated zest and juice of 1 small lemon
1/4 teaspoon ground mace or ground
    nutmeg
freshly ground black pepper
2 tablespoons finely chopped fresh
    tarragon leaves
fresh bread, to serve

Preheat the oven to 200°C/fan oven 180°C/gas mark 6. **Aga 4/3/2-door** *Grid shelf on the floor of the roasting oven.*

Place the hazelnuts on a baking tray and toast them for 2–3 minutes in the oven. Roughly chop the toasted nuts.

Beat the cheese and butter together in a medium mixing bowl with a wooden spoon until they are well blended.

Add the sherry and mix well. Stir in the cream, lemon zest and juice and mace or nutmeg.

Season with black pepper to taste, then stir in the chopped hazelnuts and chopped tarragon. Spoon the potted cheese into 4 individual ramekins or a larger serving dish.

Serve the potted cheese at room temperature with warm, freshly baked bread.

If you are not going to serve the cheese straight away, cover and chill it in the fridge for up to 5 days. Make sure you allow enough time before serving it to let it come back to room temperature.

Lotte's tips
I served this up recently on toast to a bunch of friends, with my Plum and ginger instant chutney (see page 209). It was completely delicious! The plums and ginger went brilliantly with the tarragon and hazelnuts – not a combination I would have naturally put together, but one that surprised us all by its scrumptiousness.

You can seal the cheese with some clarified butter (see Potted salmon with sorrel, page 62), as it does look lovely and will add to the flavour. However, it's not completely necessary, as nowadays we have clingfilm to do the same sealing/preserving job! The wonderful benefit of sealing with butter though, is that it makes it completely airtight and really does aid preservation.

cheesy biscuits

I've made these scrummy biscuits for years. They are so easy to make – it really is just a case of mixing a few ingredients together, chilling and baking. They are light and crispy and impossible to stop eating. Believe me, I've tried. 'Oh go on then, just one more' is my cheesy biscuit mantra!

Makes approx 40 when cut 5mm/ $^{1}/_{4}$ inch thick

110g/4oz butter, softened
110g/4oz self-raising flour
75g/3oz mature Cheddar cheese, grated
25g/1oz Parmesan cheese, grated
a pinch of cayenne pepper
1 egg, beaten
pumpkin seeds, sesame seeds,
    sunflower seeds, fennel seeds, poppy
    seeds or pine nuts, for sprinkling

Preheat the oven to 200°C/fan oven 180°C/gas mark 6. **Aga 4/3/2-door** *Grid shelf roasting oven.*

Place the butter, flour, cheeses and cayenne pepper in a food processor and whizz until they all come together to form one lump of dough.

Next place a large piece of clingfilm on the worksurface. Turn the dough onto it and roll it into a cylinder shape, about 4cm/1$^{1}/_{2}$ inches in diameter. Wrap it up and place in the fridge to chill for at least 1 hour.

Remove the dough from the fridge and take it out of the clingfilm. Use a sharp knife to slice the dough into discs, the colder the dough, the easier this is to do. If you want nice thin biscuits, cut the slices about 5mm/$^{1}/_{4}$ inch thick. The amount you get will depend on how big the cylinder was and how thick you cut the biscuits.

Place the discs onto a non-stick baking sheet and brush with the beaten egg. Sprinkle over your chosen seed toppings and bake for about 4–5 minutes in the oven until firm and golden brown.

Cool on a wire rack and then eat. I just know you won't be able to resist!

Lotte's tips
These freeze very well. Open freeze them to begin with on a wire rack and then layer them up between greaseproof paper in an airtight container. They thankfully defrost extremely quickly, so if you do make a batch or ten for the freezer, you'll always have some to pull out and eat with a cheeky gin!

candied sweet potatoes with maple syrup and wild garlic and chives

It's not unusual for me to cobble together a few ingredients and invent a new dish. There is always something lurking at the bottom of my fridge (see Plum cake page 46) that I can use, and one day in early summer it was a couple of sweet potatoes.

My Dad and Cathy, his new wife were popping by for some drinks. I thought they could nibble on some roasted sweet potatoes. So, I tossed them in a little oil and popped them in the oven. Towards the end of cooking I rooted in my cupboard, found some maple syrup and thought – why not? Back into the oven until the syrup was bubbling. Once cooked, and as they cooled the potatoes hardened up and candied. I picked some wild garlic, chopped it with chives and scattered it all over the top. The dish was finished with a flurry of chive flowers and some sea salt – perfect!

Serves 2–4

450g/1lb sweet potatoes, peeled and
   sliced into chunky chips
1½ tablespoons rapeseed oil
2 tablespoons maple syrup
a handful of sliced wild garlic leaves or
   1 tablespoon chopped fresh chives
a couple of chive flower heads,
   separated into individual flowers.
sea salt

Preheat the oven to 200°C/fan oven 180°C/gas mark 6. **Aga 4/3/2-door**
Grid shelf on floor of roasting oven.

Scatter the sweet potatoes onto a non-stick baking sheet and pour over the oil. Rub the oil all over the potatoes using your fingers so each one is covered.

Bake the potatoes for about 30 minutes until they are brown. They won't be very crispy at this stage, so don't worry. Pour the maple syrup over the potato wedges using a spoon, make sure the syrup is over all the potatoes.

Return to the oven for about 5 minutes until the maple syrup is bubbling and the sweet potatoes a little more crispy.

Remove the baking sheet from the oven. As the potatoes start to cool, they become candied and harder.

Scoop them up and transfer the potatoes to a serving dish, scatter over some sea salt, the wild garlic leaves or chives and then the flowers. These are equally delicious served warm or cold.

[A family footnote]
Cathy and my Dad recently had little Jamie. Jamie is my first brother. I was an only child for forty-two years and then this scrumptious squidge arrived. He is completely gorgeous and has a fabulous knack for making you smile. One of my Godson's, Freddie made a very funny, insightful remark when Jamie was first born. He said, 'Lotte, you don't need to worry about the fact that you are much older than Jamie. The good news is that you won't be fighting over his toys.' Oh, I don't know I'm rather partial to a toy train.

pork with green peas

Duck with green peas is a famous English dish traditionally served at Whitsun. I've had a little play with it and this is the result. Lighter, less fatty but still worthy of a Whitsun shindig.

Serves 4–6

2 tablespoons rapeseed oil
900g/2lb diced leg of pork
2 onions, cut into chunks
3 tablespoons plain flour
275ml/10fl oz medium dry cider
275ml/10fl oz chicken stock
$\frac{1}{4}$ teaspoon dried thyme
$\frac{1}{4}$ teaspoon dried sage
1 tablespoon chopped fresh parsley
1 large Webb's or English round
   lettuce, shredded
225g/8oz frozen peas
2 dessert apples, peeled and sliced
juice of 1 lemon
grated zest of $\frac{1}{2}$ lemon
5 tablespoons double cream
5 tablespoons roughly chopped fresh
   mint leaves
salt and freshly ground black pepper

Preheat the oven to 180°C/fan oven 160°C/gas mark 4.
Aga 4/3-door *Middle of baking oven.*
Aga 2-door *Grid shelf on floor of roasting oven with cold plain shelf on second runners.*

Heat the oil in a large flameproof casserole dish and fry the pork in small batches until brown. Remove from the casserole with a slotted spoon and set aside.

Add the onion to the dish and gently fry for 5 minutes until browning around the edges. Sprinkle over the flour and stir it in with a wooden spoon.

Return the meat to the pan and add the cider. Bring to the boil and simmer for 1–2 minutes, stirring the flour into the sauce with a wooden spoon to make sure there are no lumps.

Pour in the stock and add the thyme, sage and parsley. Bring up to the boil, cover and cook in the oven for 45 minutes or until the meat is tender.

Take the casserole out of the oven and add the lettuce, peas, apples and lemon juice and zest. Stir well to incorporate and return to the oven for a further 10 minutes.

Stir in the cream, season well, toss in the mint and serve.

Lotte's tips
I think this recipe is delicious served on its own in a bowl and maybe with a slice of bread or two on the side. But if you want something a bit more substantial at a dinner party, do what I sometimes do – add about 110g/4oz of halved, cooked, hot new potatoes per person to the pork about 5 minutes before the end of the cooking time.

You'll probably need a spoon to finish the sauce, as apparently it's not good manners to slurp the sauce directly from the bowl – unless of course you are on your own behind closed doors!

salmon, horseradish and beetroot on spelt pancakes

Spelt is an ancient grain, grown in Europe for millennia and with a yummy nutty flavour. It's been a tad neglected of late and nudged aside in favour of pure white flour. I feel a bit sorry for it. I love you spelt, I won't abandon you – I'll even pour you from the bag into one of my nice glass jars and give you a special label. I think you're lovely.

Makes approximately 55 pancakes

For the pancakes
2 eggs
75g/3oz plain flour
75g/3oz spelt flour
$\frac{1}{2}$ teaspoon bicarbonate soda
1 teaspoon cream of tartar
275ml/10fl oz semi-skimmed milk
salt
vegetable oil, for cooking

For the topping
4 tablespoons crème fraîche
1 medium, cooked beetroot, finely
    diced
2 teaspoons horseradish sauce
1 tablespoon snipped fresh chives
75g/3oz smoked salmon, chopped
freshly ground black pepper
thin slices of beetroot and chopped
    chives, to garnish

To make the pancakes, place the eggs in a medium mixing bowl and whisk them with a balloon whisk until frothy. Then beat in the flours, bicarbonate of soda, cream of tartar and a pinch of salt. Add half the milk and beat well, then add the other half and beat until it is nice and smooth.

Heat a little vegetable oil in a large, non-stick frying pan and pour in tablespoons of batter. Cook for a minute until the bubbles that come up start to set, then turn over and cook the other side until lightly brown. Repeat until all the batter is used up. The pancakes are served at room temperature so once cooked, they can simply be put onto a serving platter.

To make the topping, place the crème fraîche in a small mixing bowl and stir in the beetroot, horseradish and chives. Taste and season with a little black pepper. Add the salmon and gently fold in.

To serve, place a little of the salmon mixture on top of each pancake and then garnish with beetroot slices and chives.

Lotte's tips
This mixture makes a lot of pancakes, so there are plenty to freeze. You'll find that you won't use all of them up with the amount of topping this recipe gives you. I don't see the point of making a small batch each time – make plenty and then just whip them out of the freezer and onto a pan to heat through. Brilliant if you have some unexpected guests or you just fancy a snack. And, might I be so bold as to suggest a large poached or fried egg on top of a couple of them for breakfast!

homemade butter

Have you ever over-whipped your cream, turned it yellow and thought '****!!' and thrown it away? Yes so did I, before my cream epiphany whilst eating scones in Oxford with all my friends when I was 19. I was working in a local restaurant at the time and enjoying halcyon days of silliness. We would all meet up for a stodgy, sugary hangover cure in the afternoon before the evening shift. I actually don't like cream terribly, so I started fiddling with it. After stirring the little pot for a while with a small teaspoon I discovered... butter. Can you believe it? Years of living in the country, a cordon bleu cookery course and working in restaurants since I was 16 and I discovered real butter in a small white pot over an overpriced cream tea. So, the next time you just happen to over whip the cream, don't throw it away, carry on beating it and make some butter. Or just make some anyway – it's a lovely present to take to friends when visiting. Wrapped up in greaseproof paper and tied with string, it's a very different way to say thank you. I usually use this butter within a week. Sea salt helps to preserve it – and I love the crunch of salt crystals amongst the creamy butter.

Makes approximately 300g/11oz

570ml/1 pint double cream
1–2 teaspoons sea salt

Pour the cream into a mixing bowl and using an electric whisk, start beating. Keep beating until the cream starts to look like its curdling – it will turn slightly yellow.

Continue beating and you'll start to see it separating and liquid coming out of the mix. Pour this liquid off and keep. You should get about 255ml/8fl oz which you can use to make Dried berry scones (see page 80).

As you continue to beat, the mixture will start to resemble butter. The liquid will continue to come out and you need to keep pouring it off.

Stop beating with the whisk now and finish off with a wooden spoon. You need to keep pushing it about and pressing it with the back of the spoon to remove any remaining liquid.

Place the butter in a clean bowl and then beat in the salt. This will help preserve the butter a bit longer. If you prefer you can leave it unsalted.

Take a piece of greaseproof paper and spoon the butter on to it. Using the paper, shape the butter into a rectangle, wrap and then tie with some string. Store in the fridge for up to 1 week.

dried berry scones

These scones are delicious with lashings of homemade butter and my Winter tonic jelly (see page 158)

Makes 12 scones

450g/1lb self-raising flour
2 level teaspoons baking powder
110g/4oz homemade butter (see page 79)
110g/4oz chopped dried cranberries, strawberries or raspberries
3 tablespoons caster sugar
275ml/10fl oz buttermilk from the homemade butter (top it up with water to the correct measurement if necessary)
flour, for dusting
milk, for glazing
homemade butter, Winter tonic jelly or jam and clotted cream, to serve

Preheat the oven to 200°C/fan oven 180°C/gas mark 6. **Aga 4/3/2-door** *Grid shelf on the floor of roasting oven.*

Sift the flour and baking powder into a medium mixing bowl and rub the butter in with your fingertips until the mixture looks like fine breadcrumbs. Stir in the dried berries and sugar.

Add the milk and mix to form a soft, but not sticky dough.

Turn the dough out onto a floured worksurface and pat it out to about 2cm/^{3}/$_4$ inch thick. Dip a 7.5cm/3in biscuit cutter in flour and press out as many rounds as possible. Gather the trimmings together, pat the remaining dough out again and cut out more rounds.

Put the scones on a non-stick baking sheet and brush the tops with milk. Bake in the oven for about 10–12 minutes until risen and golden. Transfer to a wire rack to cool.

Split and serve with homemade butter, Winter tonic jelly or jam and clotted cream.

proper lemonade

It's a hot sultry summer's day in 1919... My darling Bertie has just finished a game of tennis with his best chum Charlie. Bertie has thrashed him and they are jesting with each other as they walk towards me. The sun catches my beautiful Bertie's golden hair and his azure blue eyes are quite arresting against his tennis whites. I feel my pulse race as he removes his boater tosses it on the blanket, sits down and stretches out his long muscular legs. We all take tea under the shade of the oak tree. There are cucumber and paste sandwiches, a light fruit cake and pink meringues. I am wilting in my corset, but make light of it when enquired as to my rosy complexion. Bertie, flushed from his exercise is thirsty. I've had Cook make some of his favourite lemonade. He winks at me and drinks it as though his thirst will never be quenched... and I drink it with a surreptitious dash of gin. What-ho Bertie!

Makes 1.2–1.7 litres/2–3 pints

450g/1lb granulated sugar
1.2 litres/2 pints boiling water
25g/1oz tartaric or citric acid (see Lotte's tips)
zest and juice of 4 lemons (see Lotte's tips)
icing sugar, to sweeten
sparkling water and ice, to serve

Pour the sugar into a bowl large enough to hold the sugar and water. Pour the boiling water over the sugar and leave to cool until it is tepid.

Now add the tartaric or citric acid and the lemon zest and juice. Stir well, cover and leave in a cool place for 24 hours.

Taste the lemonade and if you want it a bit sweeter add a little icing sugar (it dissolves much quicker than granulated).

Now bottle (see Lotte's tips) and keep it in the fridge for up to 2 weeks.

To serve, dilute with some sparkling water, I find about 55ml/2floz of lemonade to 570ml/1 pint of water works well, and top up with ice.

Lotte's tips
You can buy tartaric or citric acid from your local chemist. You may need to ask the pharmacist as they are usually kept behind the counter.

You can use any lemons for the lemonade but if you can get hold of unwaxed lemons, even better because they are not coated in preserving wax and they have a purer flavour. However, if you can't find any, not to worry – just wash the lemons in some warm soapy water, rinse and dry and then use.

It's best to store the lemonade in glass bottles as these can be sterilized (see below). I've been known to use old gin bottles! When I bring out the gin bottle at 10am on a sunny, summers morning and ask if anyone would like a drink, I do get some strange looks, until they see it's lemonade inside and not my favourite tipple!'

To sterilise glass bottles or jars
Preheat the oven to 120°C/fan oven 110°C/gas mark 1/2
Aga 4/3/2-door *Simmering oven.*

If you have a dishwasher, you can pop your bottles or jars and lids in that and wash them on a high temperature – this is enough to sterilise the jars. I usually do this, and then put them in the oven to dry them out for about 15 minutes. The bottles or jars and lids are then ready to use.

If you don't have a dishwasher, wash the bottles or jars and lids in hot soapy water, rinse and then place in a roasting tray. Boil a kettle and then pour the boiling water into the jars and bottles and over the lids. Pour the water away and then place the tray in the oven for about 15 minutes. The bottles or jars and lids are then ready to use.

june

Oh, my garden is really blooming now. It's at its very best in June, all plumped up and pleased with itself. So much colour and so many delicious roses, including my favourite variety, Raspberry Ripple, the copious shrub ones and I mustn't forget my climbing Summer Wine, Constance Spry, and the Rambling Rector...

OK, I'd better get this on the record. My name is Lotte Duncan and I am also a rose addict. There I've said it. It's so good to get it off my chest!

barbecued lamb with winter tonic jelly

I also use this recipe for barbecue or fire pit cooking (see July).

Either way, it is a fabulous way to eat lamb – tons of garden summer herbs and garlic mixed with my favourite rapeseed oil. Rapeseed has a fabulous nutty flavour, half the saturated fat of olive oil, loads of vitamin E, omega thingies and can also be heated to a very high temperature without burning. Marvellous stuff! And the best thing is, it's grown on our fair isle – my favourite comes from Yorkshire. Spread some homemade mayonnaise on a crusty roll, stuff with rocket leaves, ripe tomato, thin slices of this lamb and Bob's your shiny oyster.

Serves 8–10

2kg/4$\frac{1}{2}$lb leg of lamb, boned and butterflied (ask your butcher to do this for you)
4 tablespoons rapeseed oil
2 tablespoons chopped fresh chives
2 tablespoons chopped fresh parsley
2 tablespoons chopped fresh mint
1 tablespoon chopped fresh rosemary
8 garlic cloves, chopped
4 fresh bay leaves, halved
225g/8oz Winter tonic jelly (see page 158) or 225g/8oz redcurrant jelly
salt and freshly ground black pepper

Open the leg of lamb out and place it, skin side down, on a large tray or in a large dish.

Pour the rapeseed oil into a bowl and add the herbs, garlic and seasoning. Mix well and then pour over the lamb. Alternatively, put the oil, whole herbs and garlic and seasoning in a food processor and whizz for about 30 seconds.

Rub the herby oil all over the meat, getting it into all the crevices. Don't waste any of it, it's too good!

Cover the lamb and place it in the fridge. Leave it to marinate overnight if possible, to really flavour the meat, but if you are short of time, 2 hours will do.

Place the lamb skin side down on a ready-to-cook barbecue and cook for 25 minutes, preferably covered with a barbecue lid. If you don't have a lid, not to worry, a double layer of foil, loosely covered over the lamb will do pretty much the same job.

After this time, turn the lamb and spread the skin with half the jelly. Cover with the lid for another 20 minutes.

Take the lamb off the barbecue, glaze with a little more jelly and cover with foil. Leave in a warm place to rest for at least 10 minutes before serving.

I think the best way to serve this is to plonk it onto a large board, slice it and then let everyone tuck in.

english herb and flower salad

I love my garden and flowers so much that I want to bring their colour and fragrance into my cooking wherever possible. I can understand some people's reticence at eating a salad full of flowers. But actually we've been doing this in England for centuries. And believe it or not, as a nation we've always been big salad eaters. Take some green salad leaves; add a few crunchy vegetables and fresh herbs. Finish with some flowers and you've turned a boring green salad into an exciting, appealing, pretty dish. I grow plenty of herbs in my garden especially for this salad. You can pick most of them up at the supermarket, except for perhaps the lemon balm. Lemon balm is easily found at a garden centre and not only lovely in a salad, but also fabulous as a refreshing drink. Plant it out in the sun in a pot or soil and it will treat you to its wonderful fragrant leaves year upon year. I sometimes make myself a lemon balm infusion after a heavy meal – it really helps digestion and is anti-spasmodic. Drop about 12 washed leaves into a cup; pour over some boiling water and leave it to infuse for 5 minutes, then drink. Sorrel is also very easy to grow – simply scatter some seeds over raked soil and leave. It will come up year after year and brighten up your meals. It's a bit of a bully though, so put it somewhere where it won't take over.

Serves 6–8

For the salad
1 bulb of fennel, thinly sliced and
    tossed in lemon juice
1 bunch of watercress
approximately 250g spinach
approximately 100g rocket
a large handful of sorrel leaves, stalks
    removed and leaves shredded
1 small leek, white part only, finely
    sliced
6 spring onions, finely sliced
20 fresh mint leaves, sliced
10 lemon balm leaves, sliced (optional)
1 tablespoon chopped bronze fennel
    fronds or 1 tablespoon chopped fresh
    dill
10 nasturtium leaves

For the dressing
1 tablespoon lemon juice
2 tablespoons rapeseed oil
1 teaspoon wholegrain mustard
1 teaspoon clear honey
salt and freshly ground black pepper
edible flowers and petals, to garnish
    (see Lotte's tips)

Put all the salad ingredients into a large serving dish. Toss together.

Now, mix the lemon juice, oil and mustard together with the honey in a small jug. Season with salt and pepper and stir well to combine.

Drizzle the dressing over the salad just before serving and then scatter the flowers and petals over the top.

Lotte's tips
I love using edible flowers. The most common ones are nasturtium flowers, calendula marigolds, rose petals (use lots of different colours), blue or white borage, chive flowers, thyme flowers, rosemary flowers and lavender. All of these flowers can easily be grown in your garden. Seeds are cheap and the wonderful thing about nasturtiums and borage is that they seed themselves quite successfully the following year – especially borage – it's gone bonkers in my garden!

asparagus, goat's cheese and bacon, garden herb and flower salad

You can add lots of different things to the basic English herb and flower salad – this main course version really is a treat.

Serves 6–8 as a main course

225g/8oz dry cured streaky bacon
225g/8oz frozen soya beans
2 bunches of asparagus
2 tablespoons rapeseed oil
All the ingredients from English herb and flower salad (see page 87)
175g/6oz young, fresh, soft goat's cheese

Preheat the oven to 200°C/fan oven 180°C/gas mark 6. **Aga 4/3/2-door** *Grid shelf of the roasting oven.*

Heat a large, non-stick frying pan over a medium heat. Add the bacon and fry it until it is lovely and crispy. Blot it on some kitchen paper and then snip it into bite-size pieces using kitchen scissors. Set aside.

Bring a medium pan of water to the boil, add the soya beans and bring back to the boil. Boil the beans for 3 minutes then drain and refresh in cold, running water. Set aside.

Place the asparagus onto a large baking sheet and pour over the rapeseed oil. Cook in the oven for about 5–8 minutes depending on how thick the spears are. You want them to be cooked through, but not overcooked and soggy or too brown.

Put all the salad ingredients into a large serving dish. Toss together.

Now, mix all the dressing ingredients together in a small jug. Season with salt and pepper and stir well to combine.

Break the goat's cheese up with your fingers and dot it over the salad. Sprinkle over the bacon, soya beans and asparagus.

Drizzle the dressing over the salad and finally scatter over the edible flowers.

Lotte's tips
English Spenwood cheese is also good in this salad instead of the goat's cheese. It is a hard ewe's milk cheese not dissimilar to Pecorino. We now have more cheeses in Britain than in France, so it's really worth seeking them out and giving new ones a go.

salmon, pea and mint fishcakes with homemade tartar sauce

All I can say here is please, please, please make these fishcakes and serve them with the Tartar sauce that you've made yourself. It's one of my favourite combinations and a complete hit whenever I serve it up to friends.

Home-made tartar sauce really is so much better than shop-bought – go on give it a go, you'll never look back! I sometimes have a little tartar sauce left over (it keeps well, covered in the fridge, for about 5 days) and a naughty treat is to have it thickly spread onto some white bread, then topped with rocket, ripe tomatoes and pink roast beef. Sandwiched together and eaten on a warm, summery day in my swing seat at the bottom of my garden overlooking the fields is really one of life's rare and wonderful treats – if a little naughty!

Serves 4

450g/1lb cold cooked salmon
275g/10oz cold cooked new potatoes, in their skins
50g/2oz cold cooked peas
1 tablespoon chopped fresh parsley
3 tablespoons chopped fresh mint
2 eggs, beaten
175g/6oz white breadcrumbs
4 tablespoon rapeseed or sunflower oil, for frying
salt and freshly ground black pepper
Tartar sauce, roasted tomatoes and salad, to serve

For the tartar sauce
2 hard-boiled eggs, shelled
1 egg yolk
150ml/5fl oz sunflower oil
150ml/5fl oz rapeseed oil
1 tablespoon cider vinegar
1 tablespoon chopped fresh parsley
1 tablespoon snipped fresh chives
2 tablespoons chopped gherkin
2 tablespoons capers in brine, drained and chopped
salt and freshly ground black pepper

First, make the tartar sauce. Carefully open the hard-boiled eggs and remove the yolks. Place the yolks into a narrow-based pudding basin or bowl. (A bowl with a smaller surface area means that you are not chasing a small amount of egg yolk around inside it, it is also easier to add the oil and less likely that the mayonnaise will curdle.) Add the raw yolk to the cooked yolk and stir them together with a spoon. Add a little seasoning. Scrape the spoon and make sure all the egg yolk mix is back in the bowl.

Combine the sunflower and rapeseed oils in a jug.

Using an electric whisk, start whisking the egg yolks and add the oil very slowly, literally a drip at a time until you have poured half of it in. Now, still with the electric whisk running, pour the rest of the oil in, in a consistent thin stream. Be patient, don't rush adding the oil otherwise you'll curdle the mayonnaise (see Lotte's tips).

If the mayonnaise gets a bit thick and hard to handle, add a teaspoon or two of vinegar from the measured amount. When all the oil is added, beat in the rest of the vinegar.

Finely chop the hard-boiled egg white and add it to the mayonnaise with the herbs, gherkin and capers.

Taste and season with a little salt and pepper.

Now make the fishcakes. Break the salmon up into bite-size pieces.

Mash the potatoes and peas together in a medium mixing bowl with a fork. Add the salmon, mix in the parsley and mint and season with salt and pepper. Stir until all the ingredients are mixed well and thoroughly incorporated.

Divide the mixture into 8 and then shape into round, flat cakes. Place them on a plate, cover with clingfilm and chill in the fridge for at least 2 hours to firm up.

When you are ready to cook the fishcakes, preheat the oven to 150°C/fan oven 130°C/gas mark 2. **Aga 4/3/2-door** *Simmering oven.*

Tip the beaten eggs onto a large, flat bowl or deep plate and spread out the crumbs on another. Dip the fishcakes in the egg, covering well and then into the breadcrumbs. It is really important that you make sure the cakes are well crumbed with no gaps.

Heat the oil in a large, non-stick frying pan over a medium heat. Add the fishcakes, 4 at a time, and fry them for 6 minutes or so on each side until they are golden brown and piping hot in the middle. Drain on kitchen paper and place in the oven to keep hot while you cook the remaining fishcakes.

Serve the fishcakes with a good dollop of Tartar sauce, some oven-roasted tomatoes and salad.

Lotte's tips
Now, if your mayonnaise does decide to curdle (and this has happened to me a couple of times – once in front of a crowd at a demonstration!) you can save it. Get a clean bowl and pop a fresh egg yolk in it. Start whisking with the electric beater and start dripping in, bit by bit the curdled mix. Do this until you have finished it all up. Now add another 150ml/5fl oz of oil to the mayonnaise, in a thin stream as before until it's finished. Add the vinegar and the rest of the tartar sauce ingredients.

There is of course an alternative to all of this – go to the shops, buy a jar of mayonnaise and add the herbs, capers, cooked egg yolk and chopped white and don't tell a soul! But if you do have time and the confidence to try making your own (and I hope I've given you that) then please do try – it really is very delicious and the rapeseed oil gives the mayonnaise a lovely buttery yellow colour and taste that is green bean and asparagus-like – yum!

elderflower cordial

In early June, I start to become elderflower obsessed. As I drive past hedgerows full of those little cream fluffy flower heads, I evaluate the ditch frontage and wonder if I can stretch over them without coming a cropper. My calculations are often wrong and I do end upside down in the ditch with a bruised bottom and nettle-stung ankles, but that is all forgotten when I bring home the bounty and make the loveliest summer drink of all. For essential tips on elderflower picking, see below.

Makes approximately 3.9 litres/ 7 pints

900g/2lb granulated sugar
3.5 litres/6 pints boiling water
50g/2oz citric or tartaric acid
   (see Proper lemonade, page 83)
40 elderflower heads, unwashed
1 orange, sliced
1 lemon, sliced
sparkling water and ice, to serve

Pour the sugar into a bowl large enough to hold the sugar and water. Pour the boiling water over the sugar, stir to dissolve the sugar and leave to cool.

Add the citric or tartaric acid to the cooled liquid.

Don't wash the elderflowers or shake them too vigorously as this will remove the pollen and the pollen is where all the wonderful fragrance is held. Place the elderflowers and the sliced fruit in the water, and make sure they are submerged.

Cover the bowl with clingfilm and leave it in a cool place for 48 hours, stirring occasionally.

Lay some muslin in a colander over another large bowl. Strain the cordial through it. Transfer the cordial to sterilized bottles (see page 83) and keep in the fridge for up to a month.

To serve, dilute with some sparkling water, 55ml/2floz of cordial to 570ml/ 1 pint of water is about right, and top up with ice.

Frozen elderflower vodka

If you make a really concentrated cordial, you can add it to vodka, put it in the freezer and drink it as an after supper digestive. On its own or with a touch of tonic, it will put a smile on your face, a spring in your step and everyone will be your lovely, lovely friend!

One of my lovely, lovely friends is neighbour and fellow Hussy, Sue. We have cheeky gin Fridays. I text Sue at about 5pm and ask the simple question – 'cheeky gin Mrs?' 'Rude not to' is usually her reply and we start around 6pm. I drink a friendly gin and Sue continues her mission to work her way through my stockpile of elderflower vodka. Finally, we complete our Friday and trumpet in the weekend with a portion of fish and chips from the shop in the village. And that, dear reader, is Cheeky Gin Friday. So...

Make one batch of the elderflower cordial as above. Remove 1 litre/ 1³/4 pints of the strained cordial for the vodka and then bottle the rest as before.

Pour the measured cordial into a large bowl and add another 20 freshly picked elderflower heads. Cover and leave overnight in a cool place. Strain again. Add 3 litres/5 pints of vodka to this, mix well and then transfer to sterilized bottles (see page 83).

This one lasts quite a bit longer. In fact I still find it's quite drinkable a year later. I put a couple of bottles in the freezer and store the rest in a dark cupboard well away from Sue!

Essential advice for picking elderflowers

When you go out hunting for elderflowers, it is very important that you take note of the following:

You should attire yourself, top to toe in long, flowing, white cheesecloth, (men too) with some wild flowers in your hair.

Pick on a sunny day, so there is lots of pollen on the flowers. Back-light yourself with some summer sunshine and skip down to the elder tree with a wicker basket upon your arm.

Now, this is where it can get complicated – you have to do a pirouette, arms up, toes pointed and... smile serenely. And, again...

Face the tree, arms up and ask the spirit of Mother Elder for permission to pluck her wondrous flowers. This is compulsory; otherwise she does get very cross. Once permission has been granted (usually signalled by a light breeze), you can start to gently remove the precious flowers for your cordial

elderflower fritters with strawberry and ginger cream

This is a lovely pudding and I serve it with either a good slug of elderflower vodka or with some fresh strawberries mixed into a stem ginger cream – or both.

Serves 4–6

For the fritters
groundnut oil, for deep frying
75g/3oz self-raising flour
25g/1oz cornflour
1 egg, beaten
1 egg white, beaten
175ml/6fl oz sparkling Perry cider
20–30 elderflower heads – don't wash them as it removes the pollen, just shake gently to remove any cheeky insects!
icing sugar, to dust

For the strawberry and ginger cream
225g/8oz strawberries, hulled and quartered
1 piece preserved stem ginger in syrup, drained and chopped
275ml/10fl oz lightly whipped double cream
icing sugar, to taste

Pour enough groundnut oil into a large saucepan, so that it is one-third full. Or pour the oil into an electronic deep fryer if you have one.

Sieve the flours into a mixing bowl. Make a well in the centre, beat in the egg and egg white and gradually add the Perry cider, beating well with each addition. Beat the batter to make sure there are no lumps in it.

Fold the strawberries and chopped ginger into the cream and sweeten with a small amount of icing sugar if you want.

Heat the oil up and test it with a piece of bread to see if it is at the right temperature – if it rises to the top and browns quickly, the oil is ready.

Dip an elderflower head in the batter and gently shake any excess off – don't be rough as you don't want to pull the flowers off or remove the pollen.

Place in the oil and as soon as you do, the flowers will open out and cook very quickly. You want them to be a lovely light golden brown. Remove with a slotted spoon and drain each flower onto some kitchen paper and continue until all the flowers are cooked.

Dredge with plenty of icing sugar and serve with the strawberry and ginger cream.

a very conceited syllabub trifle (the cheaty version)

This pudding has every right to be a little full of itself. Layer upon layer of brandy, rum, creamy custard, fruit, amaretti biscuits and Madeira cake is finally topped with a smug lemon syllabub and a cluster of roses. A pud with a well deserved ego.

Serves 10

For the syllabub
grated zest and juice of 1 lemon
150ml/5fl oz dry or medium white wine
1 heaped tablespoon icing sugar
700ml/1¼ pints double cream

For the trifle
1 x 500ml carton fresh custard
grated zest of 1 large orange
1 ready-made Madeira cake or Swiss roll, thinly sliced
5 tablespoons sherry
450g/1lb raspberries
250g/9oz amaretti biscuits
5 tablespoons brandy or rum
450g/1lb strawberries, hulled and quartered
5 fresh roses, to decorate

For the syllabub, combine the lemon zest and juice, white wine and icing sugar in a small bowl. Set aside for 2 hours.

Mix the custard with the orange zest.

Place half the cake at the bottom of a 2.3 litre/4 pint deep glass serving dish and pour over the sherry. Toss the raspberries on top. Now add the amaretti biscuits, pour over the brandy or rum and place the strawberries on top. Now pour over the custard and top with the rest of the cake.

Make the syllabub by loosely whipping the cream and adding the lemon and wine mixture gradually to it. Now, just be a bit careful at this stage – when you add lemon juice to cream it does tend to thicken it quite quickly, and you want this syllabub to be the same consistency as the custard – not over-whipped and stiff. You still want some movement in it.

Spoon the syllabub over the cake, piled on top. When you are putting the trifle together, try to show the different layers throughout, this makes for a lovely tall trifle with lots of colour.

Decorate with the roses – just popped on top like a little bouquet. It turns this trifle into a centrepiece, which looks fabulous on a summer table.

Lotte's tips
I call this trifle the cheat's version because it is literally assembled in minutes from easily available ingredients. You can make your own cake and custard, but honestly, you don't need to. When this pudding is put together all the flavours merge and I really believe you can't taste the difference. And as you know, I'm all for spending time with my friends when they come for a meal, not slaving away in the kitchen.

minted new potato and pea mash

Have you noticed there's a bit of a theme running through June – peas and mint! New potatoes gently crushed with butter and cream go so beautifully with peas and mint. These potatoes are delicious with lamb or salmon. My friend Jamie demands this mash whenever he eats at my house. Yes, demands. Really demands. He threatens all sorts. I rather like my big toe, so I do as he asks.

900g/2lb new potatoes
225g/8oz frozen or fresh peas
50g/2oz butter
5 tablespoons double cream
5 tablespoons chopped fresh mint
salt and freshly ground black pepper

Place the potatoes in a large pan of salted water. Bring it to the boil and cook the potatoes until tender. This will take about 20 minutes. In the last 5 minutes of the cooking time, add the peas to the pan.

Drain the vegetables and then lightly crush the potatoes and peas together with a masher. Don't over-do it. This mash isn't smooth; you still want to have texture and the shape of the new potatoes.

Add the butter and cream and season with salt and pepper.

Finally, and just before serving, stir in the mint.

Freezing fresh herbs

I grow a lot of mint in my garden. I ignored all the warnings about planting it in a pot first, and then submerging it into the soil, and now I have feral, rampant mint. More than I can possibly use in the summer.

So, through the season I cut it back and remove the leaves. I then place the leaves into a freezer bag and pop them in the freezer. I keep topping this up throughout the summer. Once frozen the leaves become quite brittle, and if you give the bag a squash you roughly chop the mint without the need for a knife. This means that all through the winter, when it's died back I still have fresh-tasting mint. It's not pretty enough for a salad, but it's perfect for a sauce or casserole and it saves me a fortune.

If you don't grow your own mint look out for cut price bunches on offer at the supermarket or your local market and stock up for the winter too.

I often buy reduced parsley too and simply whizz it in my food processor and then freeze it in bags. That way I have instant chopped parsley whenever I want it. I have to buy parsley, because I confess to being completely useless at growing it!

If like me you have a bonkers patch of chives – pick, snip and freeze, in the same way. Fresh thyme works well too – remove the leaves from the stalks and freeze.

The only ones I've not had much luck with are tarragon, sage and basil – but, I think these are best when lovely and fresh anyway and they are also great dried.

july

I have a hammock. And through most of July, when I'm not working, you can find me in it. I place it under an apple tree for dappled shade, cover it in a blanket, add a couple of cushions and bring a book. I never get past the first page. The gentle swing of the hammock in the warm breeze and my horizontal position always sends me to sleep – without fail. I inevitably wake up an hour later, mouth open, covered in leaves and with a small amount of dribble gathered at the corner of my chin... attractive, I know.

whole salmon baked with rosemary, orange, bay and clove

I wrote this recipe down about 15 years ago and then tested it at a cookery demonstration. I do a lot of testing at my demonstration days; it's a great way to gauge reaction. I had no idea why when I came up with this dish, that my idea of mixing orange, bay, rosemary and clove with salmon would be such a happy one. It came to me out of the blue. These are unusual flavours to combine at the best of times, but my instinct paid off and this is now one of my favourite summer dishes. If you can, use a fish kettle to cook the whole salmon – you can borrow them from some supermarkets and fishmongers. If you can't get hold of one see my tip at the end of the recipe.

Serves 12

1.3kg/3lb whole salmon, descaled and gutted (ask your fishmonger to do this)
8 sprigs of fresh rosemary
8 fresh bay leaves
8 cloves
grated zest and juice of 1 orange
mayonnaise with lemon juice and black pepper and English herb and flower salad (see page 87), to serve

Thoroughly rinse the fish to remove any leftover blood and cut the tail and fins down. You can leave the head on if you want or ask the fishmonger to remove it.

Fill the fish kettle with 300ml/10fl oz of water and put the trivet in place in the kettle. Place half the rosemary on top of the grid.

Make 4 small slits, equally placed apart down the length of each side of the fish with a sharp knife. Stab each of the bay leaves with a clove and then place a leaf into each of the slits in the salmon.

Place the salmon onto the trivet in the fish kettle, scatter over the orange zest, pour over the juice place the remaining rosemary on top and cover with the lid.

Put the fish kettle on the hob (you may need to use two rings) and bring it to the boil. Simmer gently for about 30 minutes and then switch the heat off and leave the salmon in the fish kettle for another 30 minutes to allow it to gently finish cooking.

Check the salmon to see if it's cooked by gently pulling the skin back. If it still looks a bit raw, pop it back on the heat for another 15 minutes and then leave it to cool down inside the fish kettle.

Once the fish is cooked, using the handles on the trivet, lift the salmon out of the fish kettle and slide it off the trivet and onto your serving dish. Leave it to cool slightly for 10 minutes and then remove the skin with a knife and fork. Discard the skin and the cooking liquor.

Cut the fish across from top to bottom (not head to tail) to serve into portions and lift off the bones. Once you have removed all the fish from one side, turn the salmon over and do exactly the same on the other side. There might be a few stray bones so do warn people, but most of the time, the salmon does come away from the bones quite easily and you can easily spy any rogue ones!

Serve the salmon cold. I love it with some mayonnaise that has been mixed with a little lemon juice and black pepper. It also goes beautifully with my English herb and flower salad.

Lotte's tip
If you don't have a fish kettle, you can use a large roasting tin instead. Follow the recipe as above, place the salmon in the tin and cover it with foil. Cook it on the hob as above. Alternatively, preheat the oven to 180°C/fan oven 160°C/gas mark 4, bring the salmon to the boil on the hob and then bake it for 30 minutes. **Aga 4/3-door** *Middle of baking oven.* **Aga 2-door** *Grid shelf on floor of roasting oven with cold plain shelf on second runners.*

I *love* my Aga. I wept with joy the morning after I gave birth to it.

Great blobby tears of happiness, tumbled down my cheeks as coffee in hand, propped up on pillows in bed, I read *The Aga Book* by Mary Berry from cover to cover. It showed me my future - Aga food, warm kitchen and being loved by all!

Mary, Mary, what would virgin Aga owners do without you in our first week? How would we cope with all the little nuances an Aga brings into our lives? How indeed would we make the perfect cake, fluffy rice or faultless roast without your guidance? Not easily.

I have since been trained to demonstrate and teach on an Aga myself, and I now gather the occasional Aga virgin into my kitchen and show them the light. But the woman who showed us all the way in the beginning was Mary – what a lady!

So *why* when I love my Aga so much and I couldn't imagine it ever not being in my life, and I have the perfect baked potatoes, fluffy mash and flawless roast; did I dig a large hole in my garden, line it with stones and decide to cook there?

No idea really. It was a whim. I thought, is it possible to build a fire pit from instinct? Instinct that's in all of us, the intuition evolution hasn't removed. Could I build it without the many musings found on the internet? Without a manual, and with my very own brawn.

Er, well yes I could if I had the muscles of a brave young man. I didn't have one of those, so I asked Joe. He said yes. Silly boy. Joe is more used to handling a television camera than a spade. But he dug deep and recounting his days as a Neanderthal, built a pit to be proud of. A pit superior to all other pits. A pit where we could beat our chests, scamper knuckles to the ground and cook meat. MEAT!

Well... sort of anyway. Most of the time, when friends join me for a fire pit night; we just sit around it while the food cooks slowly, chatting and drinking wine. I make flatbreads and cook them on the hot bricks. Then wrap them around tender lamb, sausages or beef stew. I cook meatloaf, wrapped in foil and buried in the embers. A selection of vegetables, flavoured with garden herbs and oil are gently cooked on top and the foil keeps the aroma inside.

Most of the time we fumble around in the dark and often I trip over the wine. But we always have a lovely time and as the air chills we keep our toes warm on the surrounding stones which have heated up to a nice toasty temperature.

Early man knew what he was doing when he invented fire. He was a clever old sausage! But man also knew what he was doing when he brought fire inside, covered it in cast iron and put four doors on it. *That man really was the cleverest of all!*

See the pages that follow for the story of this summer's fire pit and recipes.

Simon, chief fire starter lit the pit early on to ensure toasty embers for cooking. It roared to life and was fed copious logs and tree bits for a few hours, which in turn produced the most accurate temperature yet. I think we may all be finally mastering the art!

Daisy, Sophie and Gemma cleared windfall apples and lay down plenty of blankets and cushions to break everyone's fall after too much wine.

Oliver arrived with guitar in hand. Well, actually with a little more than just a guitar. A sound system followed him in, carried by his brother Hugh, his sister Poppy and his father/head roadie, Chris. Oliver is an extremely talented singer. Modest and unassuming to a degree – he just picks up the guitar and sings. Later on he did a beautiful duet with Nicky and even later sang to his very own groupies. All embedded on the grass in front of him and all mesmerised by his voice.

Everyone mucked in. Nibbles and drinks were brought to the party by everyone. Flatbreads were rolled in the kitchen by anyone who just happened to be walking through. If someone was stalking the pit, they turned or checked the food.

When it came to serving, Sue went into catering mode and made sure everyone was feasting enormously. I sliced the lamb and meat shape and cooked the few remaining flatbreads in the fire. I usually do this after the meat is out. I lay foil on top of the embers and throw a flatbread or three onto it. A few minutes on each side and they are golden and ready to cuddle the meat.

Everyone settled down on the blankets and devoured the food. We followed it up with some pudding and later when the light started to dim, we all toasted marshmallows and smothered them onto chocolate digestives. An inspired idea Nicky – thank you.

And let's hear it for the little ones: Jake, my wonderful agent's little boy (completely scrumptious, with drop-dead gorgeous eye lashes and an insatiable appetite for bread sticks); Maddy (a little squidge, with a permanently surprised look on her sweet face); Olive and Alice's little sister; Jamie – my little brother (a bit of a dude; and finally Olive and Alice (they call me Lotte Cake and I call them gorgeous twinnies – they have an enormous capacity to eat anything, including garlicky, chilli olives).

Enormous thanks must also go to Ellie (head wasp catcher). Ed, Hugh, Poppy and Sam for their constant babysitting through the day and Daisy who ran around for me and got things organised.

And a final thanks to everyone else, who came, saw and drank me out of house and home.

So, you would like your own fire pit? Fire pit cooking is not an exact science. Most of the time, we have absolutely no idea what we are doing. It's a relaxed affair, where the time it takes to cook the food, only gives us more chance to drink some wine and natter. There is too much rushing around in life, and to slow down once in a while and just 'be' is a great indulgence now, where once it was the norm.

For anyone who wants to dig and cook on a fire pit, I say have a go! Dig a hole, line it with bricks or large rugged stones and light a fire. Practise makes perfect and don't give up if you incinerate everything first time. I've had some fairly hideous disasters and some remarkable triumphs. The food isn't the most important part – it's the gathering of friends and the chatting into the night that really makes the fire pit the success it is.

> *This summer's fire pit party was one of the best. Serendipity was on display in its finest form.*

pork and chorizo meat shape

Fanny, who'll you meet properly in August, had a Scottish granny called Grandma McCaffery. She was a fine Scottish lady with a few recipes up her sleeve, but a perennial favourite was a meatloaf-type dish which for no reason known to anyone was referred to as meat shape. Apparently it was a cause of much laughter in her family. I only found this out recently when I cooked the recipe in front of Fanny for the fire pit. As I was putting it together, and tenderly coaxing the meat into a rectangle; without any warning, and with uncontrollable giggles, she fell off her stool. Then weeping with laughter, and with enormous joy, exclaimed my rather splendid recipe nothing more than meat shape. Well, I tried to be decent about it and see the funny side, but if I'm honest there was a small part of me that wanted to make Fanny wear the meat shape on her head... However, being the generous human being that I am, I have decided to honour Grandma McCaffery and call my delicious, posh meatloaf-thingy a 'shape'.

Serves 6–8

900g/2lb minced pork
2 tablespoons fresh snipped chives
$1/2$–1 teaspoon dried chilli seeds, depending on how spicy you like it
$1/2$ teaspoon salt
$1/2$ teaspoon freshly ground black pepper
225g/8oz chorizo sausage, diced into 1cm/1.2 inch cubes
8 button mushrooms, finely chopped
4 garlic cloves, crushed
1 red pepper, deseeded and finely chopped
2 tablespoons chopped fresh basil
mashed potato, pitta bread or Spicy flatbreads (see page 109), to serve

Preheat the oven to 160°C/fan oven 140°C/gas mark 3. **Aga 4/3-door** *Grid shelf on floor of baking oven.* **Aga 2-door** *Grid shelf on floor of roasting oven with cold plain shelf on third runners.*

Place the minced pork in a large mixing bowl. Add the chives, chilli seeds, salt and pepper and stir well to combine.

Toss the chorizo sausage into a medium, non-stick frying pan over a medium heat. As the fat starts to run, add the mushrooms, garlic and red pepper. Cook for about 5 minutes, stirring occasionally and then set aside to cool.

If cooking the shape in an oven or Aga place half the minced pork mixture in the bottom of a 900g/2lb loaf tin (there is no need to grease it). Stir the basil into the cooled chorizo mixture and spread it on top of the pork. Top with the remaining minced pork.

Cover the loaf tin with some foil and then place it in a roasting tin. Half-fill the roasting tin with boiling water and then cook it for $1\frac{1}{2}$ hours or until it is firm to the touch. The gentle cooking in the bain marie will prevent the loaf from drying out. **Aga 4/3/2-door** *I often place the loaf in the baking oven for 30 minutes and then leave it in the simmering oven until it is cooked.*

If cooking the shape in a fire pit, place a double layer of foil on the worksurface and assemble the shape in layers on the foil as above, making sure it is rectangular. Put the meat shape on the embers and turn once. It is a more direct heat, but the foil prevents it from drying out. It will take about the same time to cook – but fire pit cooking, is not an exact science, so check it half way through!

Turn the shape out and serve as a main with some buttery mash or as a picnic food with some pitta bread, wraps or Spicy flatbreads.

spicy flatbreads

I made these the first time we ever cooked on the fire pit. Joe had just dug it out, Fanny was helping to light it and I was looking forlornly in my fridge for some food. There wasn't a lot there. So I opened the freezer and took out some diced beef, added bits and bobs to it and made a 'cowboy type' stew to cook on the pit. I had no potatoes to bake, and we'd eaten all the bread for breakfast (it wasn't looking good!). Then I remembered a scene from Michael Palin's *Around the World in 80 Days* when he was on a dhow sailing to India. The cook on the vessel made chapattis, rolling the dough out and then cooking them over a hot flame. Although he used chick pea flour, I thought a bit of self-raising might do the trick. I'd need to add some oil to help make them pliable and spices would be necessary to liven them up and pay homage to their Indian roots. Surely, if I laid some foil onto the embers and popped a rolled out flatbread on there, it would do the trick? Eureka! It did and we dined well that afternoon on beef and bean stew, spicy experimental flatbreads and fresh air. Marvellous.

Makes 8–10

450g/1lb self-raising flour
1 teaspoon chilli seeds
2 teaspoon cumin seeds
2 teaspoon fennel seeds
2 teaspoon dried cumin
3 teaspoon garam masala
4 tablespoons rapeseed oil

Put all the dry ingredients into a large mixing bowl and stir them together.

Add the oil and stir well. Next, add enough cold water to make a soft, pliable dough.

Break the dough into golf-ball sized pieces and roll the piece out on a floured board. They should be about 3mm/$\frac{1}{8}$ inch thick and 20cm/8 inch in diameter.

Heat a large, non-stick frying pan over a medium heat. Place a flatbread in the pan and cook for a couple of minutes until it is golden brown, flip and cook the other side for another 2 minutes or until golden brown. Or you can use the simmering plate on the Aga.

To cook the breads on a fire pit – lay two layers of foil on a hot brick which has been warming up under the embers. Toast each side for a few minutes until lovely and brown.

Wrap the cooked bread around meat and eat!

fire pit baked leg of lamb with my garden herbs

This is the same recipe as the Barbecued leg of lamb in June (see page 86) except we don't cook the lamb open; we wrap it in three layers of foil and place it on the embers. Half way through the cooking time I always check on it and that's when I baste it with the Winter tonic or redcurrant jelly, re-seal the foil and then continue to cook until the lamb is perfectly pink. Again, time isn't exact, but I usually give it about 1–1½ hours... or the time it takes to drink a bottle of wine! (Since I wrote the above, my lovely friends have informed me that 'a bottle' is quite ridiculous. Apparently it's more like five.) Slices of this lamb inside the flatbreads with perhaps some mayonnaise and leaves of rocket are more delicious than I can possibly describe! So, I won't – you'll just have to make it. You can also cook this lamb in a more conventional way – in an oven!

Preheat the oven to 200°C/fan oven 180°C/gas mark 6. **Aga 4/3/2-door** *Grid shelf on the floor of the roasting oven.*

Place the lamb in a large roasting tin and cover it with foil. Cook for 45 minutes and then remove the foil. Return to the oven for another 20 minutes and then remove. Replace the foil and leave to rest somewhere warm for 20–30 minutes.

cheesy mustard, ham and chive pull-apart bread

I love *Australian Woman's Weekly* recipes. In fact I love lots of things about Australia. Never been there mind, but hope to someday soon.
As I was flicking through the magazine with my friend Jacqueline, she noticed a dish called Apple Pull Apart.
We made it and it was really rather nice. But I decided to have a play and turn it into a savoury bread (just to be awkward) and this is the result.

Makes one 23cm/9-inch round loaf

butter, for greasing
225g/8oz self-raising flour
25g/1oz butter
3 tablespoons snipped fresh chives
200ml/7fl oz semi-skimmed milk
flour, for dusting
1 tablespoon wholegrain mustard
2 teaspoons Dijon mustard
110g/4oz ham, finely chopped
110g/4oz mature Cheddar cheese, grated
1 egg, beaten

Preheat the oven to 200°C/fan oven 180°C/gas mark 6. **Aga 4/3/2-door** *Grid shelf on floor of roasting oven.*

Grease a deep 23cm/9-inch round cake tin with the butter

Sieve the flour into a medium mixing bowl and rub in the 25g/1oz of butter.

Mix in 1 tablespoon of the chives, and then gradually stir in just enough milk to form a soft, sticky dough.

Turn the dough out onto a floured worksurface and knead it until it is smooth. Roll it out to form a 25x30cm/10x12 inch rectangle.

Spread the dough with the mustards and then sprinkle with the remaining chopped fresh chives, the ham and finally the cheese, to within 2.5cm/1 inch of the long edge, but right up to the edge of the short one.

Roll the dough up like a Swiss roll. Use a floured serrated knife to cut it into 16 slices. Place 10 slices upright around the edge of the cake tin and 6 in the middle. Brush the top with the beaten egg to glaze. Place the cake tin on a baking sheet.

Bake in the oven for about 15–20 minutes, until golden brown.

Leave in the tin for a few minutes before turning onto a wire rack to cool.

Lotte's tips
This is a wonderful, quick recipe and a very social bread – you pass it around and everyone just pulls it aparrrt!

Eat it warm, not too hot as it's a bit too doughy straight after cooking and it needs time to settle a little.

vegetables and herbs in foil

You can buy vegetables especially for this recipe or you can just use whatever you have around your kitchen. I first did this with odds and sods from my vegetable patch. Honestly – anything goes. This is one of those dishes that doesn't really have any parameters – just go for it!

Serves 4–6 (depending on how many veg you use!!)

olive oil
a selection of various summer
    vegetables such as:
carrots, thinly sliced
courgettes, cut into chunks
red, yellow and green peppers,
    deseeded and cut into chunks
onions, sliced
garlic, sliced
new potatoes, halved
sweetcorn, sliced into wedges
beetroot, cut into chunks
lots of fresh herbs such as:
parsley
chives
marjoram
oregano
rosemary
salt and freshly ground black pepper

Preheat the oven to 180°C/fan oven 160°C/gas mark 4. **Aga 4/3-door** *Middle of the baking oven.* **Aga 2-door** *Grid shelf on the floor of the roasting oven with cold plain shelf on second runners.*

Place 2 large sheets of foil on top of each other and drizzle some olive oil over.

Scatter the vegetables over the foil and then season with salt and pepper. Drizzle over some more oil.

Toss the herbs on top and then fold the foil over and seal the edges tightly.

Cook the parcel in the oven for about 45–60 minutes. Or you can cook the vegetables on the fire pit – and once again you just have to wait and check until it's cooked – but this does give you plenty of time to enjoy the wine!

sausage and bean casserole

I serve this casserole as a backup dish for fire pit days – just in case I set fire to the meat or surrounding shrubs! And I must say it is equally as good on a non fire pit day. Just pop everything in the casserole, then the oven and go to the pub while it cooks.

Serves 4

4 tablespoons olive oil
900g/2lb good-quality sausages, cut into chunks
2 large onions, finely chopped
3 carrots, diced
1 small red chilli, deseeded and chopped
1 whole bulb of garlic, halved widthways
1 tablespoon balsamic vinegar
570ml/1 pint red wine
4 sprigs of fresh rosemary
2 bay leaves
250g can chopped tomatoes
250g can brown or Puy lentils, drained
250g can cannellini beans
250g can borlotti beans
570ml/1 pint chicken or vegetable stock
1 tablespoon Dijon mustard
salt and freshly ground black pepper
mashed potatoes or crusty bread, to serve

Preheat the oven to 160°C/fan oven 140°C/gas mark 3. **Aga 4/3-door** *Grid shelf on floor of baking oven.* **Aga 2-door** *Grid shelf on floor of roasting oven with cold plain shelf on third runners.*

Heat the oil in a large flameproof casserole dish over a medium heat. Add the sausage chunks and brown them in the oil, remove from the pan and set aside.

Add the onions, carrots, and chilli to the dish. Cook over a gentle heat for 10 minutes, stirring occasionally.

Now pop in both halves of the garlic bulb and the balsamic vinegar. Follow this with the wine, rosemary and bay leaves. Bring up to the boil and then simmer to reduce the liquid by half.

Add the tomatoes, lentils, beans, stock and mustard to the dish. Now, pop the sausage chunks back in, bring it all to the boil and simmer for 5 minutes. Cover the casserole and place in the oven to cook for $1\frac{1}{2}$ hours.

Before serving, season with some salt and pepper to taste. Serve in bowls at the fire pit or perhaps with some mash or bread on a chilly day.

salmon, orange and bronze fennel pate

This dish is a great way to use up any leftover salmon from the Whole Salmon Baked with Rosemary, Orange, Bay and Clove recipe on page 103 and is completely yummy on top of toast or fresh doughy bread. I have lots of bronze fennel in my garden – it's seeded itself everywhere and is so pretty with its dark green stalks and aubergine coloured fronds and frills. But if you don't have any, don't worry you can use dill or tarragon.

Serves 6–8

450g/1lb cooked salmon, skinned and
  pin-boned
2 tablespoons finely chopped bronze
  fennel, dill or tarragon
zest of 1 orange
200g/7oz cream cheese
75g/3oz smoked salmon, chopped
salt and freshly ground black pepper
toast or fresh bread, to serve

Break the salmon into chunks and put it in a large mixing bowl. Add the bronze fennel, orange zest and cream cheese and work it together with a wooden spoon. Season with a little salt and pepper and stir in the chopped smoked salmon.

Adjust the seasoning to taste and spoon into a serving dish. Cover and chill in the fridge for 1 hour before serving with toast or fresh bread.

117 july

raspberry and rosewater cream tart

This is an easy peasy, light summer pudding which is so pretty and effortless to make – especially if you don't bother making the pastry at all and buy a ready-made pastry case. Did I really just say that?!

Serves 6–8

For the pastry
175g/6oz plain flour
75g/3oz butter, softened
75g/3oz sugar
3 egg yolks
a drop of vanilla extract
1 egg white
flour, for dusting

For the filling
275ml/10fl oz double cream
250g/9oz Greek yogurt
½ teaspoon rosewater
1–2 tablespoons icing sugar, to taste
450g/1lb raspberries
3 tablespoons seedless raspberry jam
pink or red rose petals, to decorate

Preheat the oven to 190°C/fan oven 170°C/gas mark 5. **Aga 4/3-door** *Top of baking oven.* **Aga 2-door** *Grid shelf on floor of roasting oven.*

To make the pastry in a food processor, put the flour, butter, sugar, egg yolks and vanilla extract into a food processor and whizz until it forms a smooth ball of dough. This may take a couple of minutes. Remove the dough from the food processor and wrap it in clingfilm. Set aside to rest in the fridge for 30 minutes.

To make the pastry by hand, sieve the flour into a large mixing bowl, make a well in the centre and then pop the softened butter, sugar, egg yolks, and vanilla extract into it. Using the fingertips of one hand, squidge the butter, sugar, egg yolks and extract together until it forms a paste. Now, slowly with your other hand, start to add the flour bit by bit until it is all incorporated into the paste. Turn onto a floured board and knead together for a minute or so, then wrap it in clingfilm. Chill in the fridge for 30 minutes.

Dust a worksurface with flour and roll out the pastry to a circle big enough to line a 23cm/9-inch loose-based flan tin. Keep the pastry hanging over the edges. Press it firmly into the base and sides, then prick the surface lightly with a fork. Now loosely beat the egg white and brush it over the surface of the pastry – this helps to seal it. Place on a baking sheet and pop it back into the fridge to chill for 10 minutes.

Bake the pastry case for 10 minutes or until it is a light golden brown. Transfer to a wire rack to cool. When cool, remove the pastry left hanging over the edges of the tin, it should break off easily and leave the edges nice and neat. Finish trimming the edges neatly with a serrated knife. Leaving the pastry hanging over the edge before cooking prevents it from collapsing back into the tin and leaves the tin perfectly lined.

Pour the cream into a medium mixing bowl and lightly whip it. Gently stir in the yogurt and rosewater and enough icing sugar to sweeten to your taste.

Crush half the raspberries and fold them into the creamy yogurt. Spoon the filling into the pastry case. Scatter over the rest of the raspberries and chill in the fridge for 15 minutes.

Heat the raspberry jam in a small pan and gently bring it to the boil. Spoon it over the raspberries and leave to set for a couple of minutes.

Finally, scatter over some pink or red rose petals. Serve within an hour or the pastry will go soggy!

baked strawberry and lavender cheesecake

Although as a nation we've used flowers in cooking for literally hundreds of years, when I first came up with this recipe the idea of using them had faded from most people's memory. They just didn't understand why I was putting edible flowers in my salads and puddings and using them as decorations. They plainly thought I was bonkers. And they'd be right – though not always because of my edible flower obsession! Strawberries and lavender are excellent soul mates, but be a little sparing with the lavender as it can be very over-powering when first picked – brimming with the lovely essential oils we so love and quite pungent. You only need a few heads to flavour the sugar.

Serves 6–8

75g/3oz caster sugar
3 fresh lavender heads, rinsed and
   dried
275g/10oz self-raising flour
50g/2oz cornflour
200g/7oz butter
1 tablespoon semi-skimmed milk
flour, for dusting
175g/6oz strawberries, hulled and
   sliced
250g/9oz curd cheese
4 large eggs, separated
150ml/5fl oz double cream
fresh lavender flowers and
   strawberries, to decorate
icing sugar, to dust

Preheat the oven to 200°C/fan oven 180°C/gas mark 6. **Aga 4/3/2-door** *Grid shelf on bottom of roasting oven.*

Put the caster sugar in a food processor. Pick the flowers off the head of lavender and add them to the sugar. Whizz together until the flowers are very fine. If you don't have a food processor, you can use a pestle and mortar to grind the flowers and sugar.

Sieve the flowers out of the sugar. You'll find that the lavender oil has flavoured the sugar quite nicely.

Now make the pastry. Sift the flours into a medium mixing bowl and rub in the butter until the mixture resembles breadcrumbs. Add enough milk to a firm but not sticky dough. Wrap the pastry in clingfilm and leave it to rest in the fridge for 30 minutes.

Dust a worksurface with flour and roll the pastry out to a circle large enough to line a 23cm/9-inch round springform cake tin. Leave the edges of the pastry hanging over the tin, this helps to prevent the pastry collapsing back into it. Chill in the fridge for 30 minutes.

Line the pastry case with greaseproof paper and baking beans and bake it blind in the oven for 10 minutes. Gently remove the beans and paper and return to the oven for 5 minutes to dry out. Now place the tin on a baking sheet. Reduce the temperature of the oven to 160°C/fan oven 140°C/gas mark 3, **Aga 4/3-door** *Grid shelf on floor of baking oven,* **Aga 2-door** *Grid shelf on floor of roasting oven with cold plain shelf on third runners.*

Arrange the strawberry slices over the bottom of the pastry case. Place the cheese, lavender sugar, egg yolks and cream in a large mixing bowl and mix them together.

Place the egg whites in a medium mixing bowl and whisk them until they are stiff. Using a metal spoon, fold a spoonful of the egg whites into the cheese mixture to soften it, and then gently fold the rest of it in.

Pour the mixture over the top of the strawberries and bake for 45–50 minutes or until firm and not wobbly in the middle. If it browns too much before it's set, cover it with some foil. **Aga 4/3/2-door** *I often pop it into the simmering over after 30 minutes and leave it there until it has set.* Remove the excess pastry that was over hanging the edge of the tin – break it off gently or use a serrated knife to tease it away.

Serve warm, decorated with the fresh lavender flowers and strawberries and dusted with some icing sugar.

Lotte's tips
If you want to make a bigger batch of lavender sugar it will keep for up to three months in an airtight container. If you leave it much longer than this, I find it tastes a little dusty and stale, the smell starts to fade and it becomes just a little bit like pot pourri!

august

Still in my hammock. But under the damson tree now. The sun has shifted position in the summer sky. Still asleep. Probably still dribbling.

And still very happy.

I've always rather hankered after the Georgian existence.

A life with Mr Darcy, dressed in his billowing white shirt and rather tight trousers, (a slight pause whilst I fan myself) in a stately pile deep in the Shropshire hills.

Aaah, Mr Darcy, smouldering away in the corner and looking upon me with love in his eyes, and possibly just a hint of lust! I'm there in my empire-line dress, curls gathered into ribbon and flushed from love's young dream.

Sigh...

Now I share this love of all things Georgian with another fabulous friend of mine – Sarah. Such is our devotion to Mr Darcy that we have this ill-conceived illusion that we are modern day Jane Austens and on occasion, pen missives to each other.

Here are a couple of our letters – very silly, perhaps a tad indulgent but great fun to do nonetheless. By the way, Sarah's pseudonym is Fanny. Mine is Martha.

The Very Rich Personages Club, Kensington

Dearest Sister,

Bath was simply marvellous. So calming to take its waters once again and it does the Colonel so much good. We are now, as you will have established, staying at his London Club.

I must own, I find city life rather too grey and busy for my liking but it is so pleasing to have the freedom to call upon one's London companions. We shall be departing for the countryside tomorrow. Not so arduous a journey as one might imagine.

Oh how I thrilled at our delightful sojourn with your dearest self. Always so hospitable, so companionable and with, as I always say, the finest cook in the country. You must endeavour to keep her on at all costs. This talk of her moving to London for some QC or other is most distressing and must be discouraged at once. Do your utmost my dear.

Another point which held my peculiar interest was that regarding the health of Miss Honey. Her recovery from such a dreadful wasting illness is indeed remarkable. I own, in fact, to never having seen anything quite like it. Do continue your special regard for her. I feel she needs to be directed carefully and yours is just the hand to do it.

By the time this reaches your fair hand you will have returned from your visit to Lady Bingley, I do hope you enjoyed it and look forward to hearing of it and your financial recompense at your earliest convenience.

Your room shall be waiting for you as ever upon your arrival in April. We look forward to it my dear and may even retrieve some wine from the cellar. Once more, so many thanks for your kind attention.

As ever, yours affectionately

Fanny

Cooks Cottage, Buckinghamshire

My dearest sister,

Once again, I find myself sitting at my writing desk, parchment in place, and quill in hand to regale you with some joyful news.

I do believe that the Colonel himself will too be overjoyed. Do please send my regards to your father, and wish him well. I am pleased indeed that his distress has been soothed so well in Bath.

My short trip to Worcestershire was as successful as it was agreeable to my purse. Indeed, I am now able to oblige my many future social arrangements and connections. Lady Bingley greeted Miss Honey and I with deep affection, as if we had known each other as cousins for many years, and Lord Bingley was disposed to take very kind proper notice of Miss Honey.

A rather grand carriage arrived

early at my cottage. Not early enough to miss the eyes of my neighbours and make us the centre of enviable gossip. This carriage, I am to make known to you, belongs to Lord and Lady Bingley. I have to confess that we did have a slightly worrying moment on our journey. I only wish that Miss Honey's propensity to carry a little more weight than is proper hadn't caused the carriage wheel to fall off.

However, with great luck and fortitude we were only delayed for a short while and arrived in Worcester for a light supper. I fear I am so caught up with our journey, that I am not telling you of my joyful news. Gossip has reached me and has put me in such a glow. Rumour that left us all so very vexed regarding my cook leaving to work for Lady Saunders, is just that my dear, rumour.

I believe the contemptible Lady Saunders and her odious husband, both of disagreeable character, started this nonsense without thought or consequence of my feelings. It has left me with nerves in tatters. Miss Honey too has suffered terribly at the thought that the finest cook in the land might be taking her leave of us. So much so, dear sister, that she has taken to her bed, and is, as I write to you reclining gently upon her pillow.

Fanny dear, on another most important note, you must call on the Bingleys when next in Worcestershire. They are known to Lord Dashwood. You are aware of his kind regard for you, since you glanced at each other at the assembly rooms last month.

I shamefully own to having listened at the Bingley's door for gossip regarding Lord Dashwood. T'would be a great pleasure to see your face as I recall the conversation. I have knowledge that his nature is open and full of charm. He is a man of good character and humour. Sister, do not delay. Please spend all but a short time in Kensington, enjoy society and then make haste to Worcestershire.

I will say no more about it Fanny until we meet. I own to a character unable to conceal my emotions or excitement for long. Do write me with news until I am able to call on you in April.

London is so pretty in the spring with its avenues of blossom. I do believe that society is quite at its best with the optimism of warmer days ahead. I do hope that your time in the Kensington countryside is both enjoyable as it is diverting.

The Colonel and you must not trouble your dear selves with talk of opening the cellar. I do not wish to be an encumbrance. Just a small glass of sack to fortify me is all I require.

With deep affection

Martha

You see? We both belong there. The only problem is, it could get quite messy if we ever decided to fight to the death over Mr Darcy

The Georgians loved a jelly. And I do believe that Fanny and Martha, faced with the wobbly delight over the page, would indeed have been highly diverted!

126 Lotte's Country Kitchen

wobbly jelly with summer fruits and flowers

I made this wobbly jelly recipe up one summer's afternoon for an impromptu barbecue at my neighbours Robyn and Simon. Later, we all wobbled home, luckily I didn't wobble into my peonies! My path is old, bumpy and rickety and you always run the chance of destroying a perennial or two when arriving home in the dark and full of wine. And just when you think you are safely up the path, you are subsequently attacked by suicidal moths hurtling themselves at the outside light as you fumble for the key. Much arm waving, dodging and general panic ensues as you drop the keys, pierce your head with the climbing rose on the wall and eventually stumble through the door skidding straight into a dead mouse the wretched Woozle has brought home.

approximately 8 leaves of gelatine (see Lotte's tips)
750ml bottle sparkling pink wine
150ml/5fl oz sloe gin
5 heaped tablespoons caster sugar
150g/5oz blueberries
150g/5oz raspberries
150g/5oz strawberries, quartered
a selection of edible flowers, to decorate
single cream, to serve

Soak the gelatine for 5 minutes in a bowl of cold water.

Pour the wine and sloe gin into a medium pan and heat very gently. Add the sugar and stir to dissolve.

Remove the gelatine leaves from the water and squeeze, with your hands, to remove any excess water. Add the soaked gelatine leaves to the wine syrup and stir over a gentle heat until dissolved.

Pop the fruit into a 1.2litre/2 pint ring mould and then pour in the wine syrup. Cover and leave to cool down a bit and then place in the fridge for at least 5 hours to set.

When you want to turn the jelly out, dip the mould carefully in another large bowl of hot water for about 2–3 seconds until you start to see it melt and loosen around the edges. Be careful not to leave it in too long. Put a plate on top of the mould and invert. The jelly should come away quite easily.

Decorate the top with a selection of edible flowers – I've used tiny bronze fennel flowers and borage on mine and serve with single cream.

Lotte's tips
Leaf gelatine comes in different sizes so do read the instructions of the particular leaf gelatine you buy, and then check how much you need for the amount of liquid used in this recipe (900ml/33fl oz).

This isn't the cheapest pudding in the book, but it's perfect for a special occasion and really worth the price of a bottle of sparkling pink wine.

salmon, leek and spinach lasagne

Jacqueline – remember her? My friend who comes for cooking lessons, but doesn't actually need them – asked me for a lower fat, healthy recipe that involved lasagne and fish. Never one to shy away from a challenge – I came up with this!

Serves 4–6

butter, for greasing
450g/1lb cooked salmon, skinned, pin-boned and flaked
1 medium leek, sliced and steamed for 2 minutes
40g/1½oz butter
40g/1½oz plain flour
570ml/1 pint skimmed milk
1 fresh bay leaf
110g/4oz half-fat mature Cheddar cheese, grated
1 tablespoon wholegrain mustard
250g/9oz frozen spinach, defrosted and pressed through a sieve
2 tablespoons chopped fresh parsley
200g/7oz canned or frozen sweetcorn (no need to thaw)
175g/6oz fresh lasagne
50g/2oz Parmesan cheese, grated
salt and freshly ground black pepper
green salad and French bread, to serve

Preheat the oven to 180°C/fan oven 160°C/gas mark 4. **Aga 4/3-door** *Middle of baking oven.* **Aga 2-door** *Grid shelf on floor of roasting oven with cold plain shelf on second runners.*

Lightly grease a 1.7 litre/3 pint lasagne dish.

Mix the salmon and leek together in a medium bowl.

Melt the butter in a small pan and stir in the flour using a wooden spoon. Remove the pan from the heat and gradually add the milk, stirring well after each addition. When you've added all the milk, return the pan to the heat, pop in the bay leaf and bring the sauce to the boil, stirring all the time. If it gets a bit lumpy, whisk it. Simmer the sauce for 1 minute. The sauce might seem a bit runny at this stage, but don't worry, the cheese soon thickens it up.

Stir in the Cheddar cheese and mustard and season. Now add the spinach, parsley and sweetcorn (including the liquid from the can). Remove the bay leaf. Gently stir in the salmon and the leeks, taste and adjust the seasoning if necessary.

Spoon a quarter of the sauce into the dish. Cover with a third of the lasagne, add another quarter of the sauce and layer with more lasagne and continue, finally finishing with a layer of the sauce. Sprinkle over the Parmesan and cook in the oven for 35–45 minutes or until golden brown and bubbling.

Serve the lasagne with a green salad and crusty French bread.

raspberry vinegar

This was originally a fragrant drink traditionally made in the country each summer. It was diluted with water to drink as a cordial, or used to soothe children's sore throats, and was also extremely popular poured over plain batter puddings. I mix mine with fizzy water and the fresh summer flavour is perfect to revive you during a long dark winter. I also use it in salad dressings and it quite delicious drizzled over some cos lettuce and rocket with cooked duck or chicken liver and bacon.

Makes approximately 570ml/1 pint

900g/2lb raspberries
570ml/1 pint white malt vinegar
450g/1lb caster sugar

Put the raspberries into a bowl and mash well with a fork. Pour the vinegar over the raspberries and cover with clingfilm. Leave for 2 days in a cool, dark place, stirring occasionally.

Strain the raspberries and vinegar through a jelly bag (see Lotte's tips) and leave to drip for an hour.

Put the sugar and strained juice into a preserving pan and stir them gently over a low heat until the sugar has dissolved. Boil gently for 10 minutes, removing the scum as it rises up.

Leave to cool and then pour into sterilized bottles (see page 83). Store in a cool dark place for up to 1 year.

Lotte's tips
If you don't' have a jelly bag you can strain the raspberries and vinegar through a piece of muslin draped over a colander instead.

greek lamb burgers with feta

These were first devised for a cookery show: 'Lotte, do you have a twist on the burger?' (Much eye rolling and muttering from me with my hand over the phone – why has there always got to be a twist?) 'Absolutely no problem at all – why don't we use minced lamb for a change, season it, shape it and shove some feta in?' Silence. Bit of nail biting my end. 'Lovely idea Lotte, let's do it.' Phew. My grumbling aside, these burgers were a great hit. They DO twist the old burger into something new and are great for a barbecue or just in a griddle pan on the hob.

Makes 6 burgers

For the burgers
900g/2lb minced lamb
4 garlic cloves, crushed
3 tablespoons chopped fresh mint
1 teaspoon dried thyme
75g/3oz pitted black olives, chopped
2 tablespoons tomato purée
50g/2oz feta cheese, cut into 6 pieces
salt and freshly ground black pepper

For the salad
1 cucumber, peeled and thinly sliced
4 tomatoes, diced
1 red onion, chopped
110g/4oz pitted black olives
$\frac{1}{2}$ teaspoon dried thyme
3 tablespoons olive oil
1 tablespoon cider vinegar
1 teaspoon clear honey

To serve
1 garlic clove, halved
6 thick slices of rustic bread
olive oil, for drizzling and cooking
2 heaped tablespoons mayonnaise

Put all the ingredients for the burgers, apart from the feta, in a mixing bowl and bring together. Mix well.

Divide the mixture into 6 equal portions. Take one portion into your hand and roll it into a ball. Flatten it out, put a piece of the feta in the middle and then draw the meat up around it. Make sure the cheese is secure within the meat. Repeat with the other 5 burgers and then place in the fridge for 10 minutes.

In the meantime, make the salad by mixing the cucumber, tomatoes, red onion, olives and dried thyme together in a large bowl and season with black pepper. Blend the olive oil, vinegar and honey together and pour over the salad.

Rub the halved garlic cloves over each slice of bread and sprinkle with a little olive oil. Heat a griddle pan over a medium heat and cook the bread on both sides until brown.

Add 1 teaspoon of oil to the griddle pan and cook the burgers, for about 8–10 minutes on each side. Stick a knife in the middle and if it comes out hot, they are cooked through. If not, continue to cook until they are.

To serve spread the mayonnaise on the toasted bread, top with a burger and then spoon over some of the salad – serve the rest on the side.

raspberry meringue fool with rosewater biscuits

I'd love to be able to give myself all the credit for this pudding. But I can't. It's based on a Cordon Bleu creation by the indomitable and rather scary late Muriel Downes. I say scary only because she petrified me. I'm sure if you weren't a slightly vacuous student, with a disregard for Cordon Bleu ways and an attitude that you knew better – you wouldn't have been quite as terrified as me.I came up against her once on how to cut an avocado for Avocado à la Greque – it was a very silly thing to do. She won. I'm not entirely sure I've ever recovered. So, this delicious pudding is fundamentally Cordon Bleu, however I really wanted to put it in my book because it's been one of the dishes that have formed that old backbone I mentioned in the introduction. It's always been there. It's never let me down. I'm passing it on to you now, so please treat it with a little respect. Otherwise I'll pay you a visit, wearing the Ms. Downes glare I've perfected so well over the years! Just in case she's listening from above, I should really tell you that I happen to know Muriel was actually a fabulously fun, incredibly knowledgeable woman who was enormously respected throughout the culinary world. I was very lucky to be taught by her, even though I didn't know that at the time! Serve the fool with the delicious Rosewater biscuits – heaven!

Serves 4–6

700g/1½ lb raspberries
3 egg whites
175g/6oz caster sugar
425ml/15fl oz double cream
Rosewater biscuits, to serve

Blend the raspberries to a purée in a food processor. Push the purée through a sieve to remove the seeds. Discard the seeds. Pour the purée into a small plastic container and then place this in the freezer overnight.

The next day, place the egg whites in a medium mixing bowl and whisk them with an electric whisk, until stiff. Then add the sugar, 1 tablespoon at a time. Continue beating until the mixture firms up again.

Place the cream in a medium mixing bowl and whisk it lightly until it is the same consistency as the egg whites.

Remove the purée from the freezer and whizz it in a food processor for just a few seconds until it separates into crystals. Or bash it with a wooden spoon in a bowl. You don't want to make a mush though.

Fold the cream and egg whites together and then quickly, but carefully, fold in the semi-frozen raspberry purée using a metal spoon.

Pile the fool into tall glasses or a glass bowl and keep in the coolest part of the fridge. Serve within 1 hour, accompanied by the Rosewater biscuits.

Lotte's tips
I remember the first fool I ever ate. It was the very hot summer of 1976 and my mum made me gooseberry fool. I ate the whole bowl. I then ate my mum's and my dad's and proceeded to polish off the spare one in the fridge. Safe to say I love a fool – useful in life as you do come across rather a lot of them...

Rosewater biscuits

Rosewater biscuits and raspberry meringue fool. True love.

Makes 12

oil, for greasing
125g/4½oz butter, softened
50g/2oz caster sugar
125g/4½oz self-raising flour
a few drops of rosewater

Preheat the oven to 180°C/fan oven 160°C/gas mark 4. **Aga 4/3-door** *Middle of baking oven.* **Aga 2-door** *Grid shelf on floor of roasting oven with cold plain shelf on second runners.*

Oil 2 baking sheets.

Place the butter and sugar in a bowl and beat them together until pale and fluffy.

Add the flour and rosewater and beat until a stiff dough forms.

Break off 12 small pieces of dough and roll them into balls, about 5cm/2 inches in diameter. Place the balls on the oiled baking sheets, making sure they are well spaced apart and flatten them gently.

Bake at for 10–15 minutes until light golden in colour. Transfer to a wire rack to cool.

These will keep for 3–4 days in an airtight container.

light fruit cake with pecans and coconut

Cooks Cottage, Buckinghamshire

Dearest Fanny,

I am in such a glow. I have discovered, much to the grievance of other ladies in London society, a cake of such fine quality as to bewitch Mr Darcy.

I have good information, having acquired it from your dear sister Jane, that Mr Darcy has been indisposed for almost a fortnight in Devonshire, with an illness that has left him quite weak.

Do you think dear sister, if I travelled to Devonshire myself with my discovery, and fed Mr Darcy the finest cake in the land, that I would indeed have his love declared upon myself?

I do fear he may be much altered, but I will not suppose it possible and hope that my darling love will still be full of affection and confidence towards me.

Oh Fanny dear, I know you will be greatly astonished by my urgency to visit him but I own to having such love and fear any more delay would not end with my hand in marriage.

Please forgive me sister, but it's every woman for herself.

With great affection and faster horses,

Martha

Well if the lovely Mr Darcy was bewitched by this cake and proposed marriage to Martha, then it really must be something special. Go on, bake it and take it to the love of your life and see if it works for you!

Makes one 20cm/8 inch cake

butter, for greasing
175g/6oz butter, softened
175g/6oz caster sugar
3 large eggs, beaten
250g/9oz self-raising flour
175g/6oz sultanas
175g/6oz currants
50g/2oz chopped pecan nuts
25g/1oz desiccated coconut
demerara sugar, for dusting

Preheat the oven to 160°C/fan oven 140°C/gas mark 3. **Aga 4/3-door** *Grid shelf on the floor of baking oven.* **Aga 2-door** *Grid shelf on floor of roasting oven with cold plain shelf on third runners or use a pre-heated cake baker. I often start the cake in the baking/roasting and then finish off for the last hour in the simmering oven.*

Grease and line a round 20cm/8-inch cake tin.

Place the butter and sugar in a medium mixing bowl and cream them together until they are pale and fluffy. Gradually beat the eggs into the mixture. Don't worry if it looks a bit curdled, it doesn't matter at all. Now fold in the flour, followed by the rest of the ingredients.

Spoon the mixture into the cake tin and bake for between 1¼–1½ hours. After 30 minutes, cover the cake with a piece of foil to prevent it from browning too much. To check if the cake is cooked, insert a sharp knife or skewer into the centre of the cake – if it comes out clean, it is cooked.

Remove the cake from the oven and leave it to cool in the tin for 10 minutes. Turn out onto a wire rack to cool completely and dust with Demerara sugar.

roasted baby new potatoes with summer herbs

I think this is such a lovely way to serve new potatoes. You can only eat them boiled or steamed with mint for so long, and then it gets REALLY boring. So, roast them and toss them in some fresh summer herbs and serve them alongside – well anything really. I've even been known to serve these up as little nibbles with wine, on a summer's evening in the garden.

Serves 6–8

2 tablespoons rapeseed oil
900g/2lb oven-sized baby new potatoes
1 large sprig of rosemary, leaves
   stripped off
1 tablespoon snipped fresh chives
1 tablespoon chopped fresh mint
1 tablespoon chopped fresh parsley
salt and freshly ground black pepper

Preheat the oven to 220°C/fan oven 200°C/gas mark 7. **Aga 4/3/2-door** *Lower roasting oven.*

Rub the oil into the potatoes with your hands and place them in a roasting tin. Sprinkle over the rosemary leaves.

Roast in the oven for 45 minutes or until golden brown. Remove from the oven a couple of times during cooking to give them a shake.

When cooked and at the last minute just before serving, stir in all the herbs and season with salt and pepper. The heat of the potatoes will wilt the herbs and release their scent immediately giving the potatoes a lovely fresh taste.

crunchy nutty chicken for nibbles with chilli jam

Sometime in late 2008 I was a little frantic with work. Demonstrations were pending, dishes needed testing, a food fair in Ireland was on the cards and a couple of big clients were after some recipes! I was frazzled to say the least. The phone rang and a very nice producer from a Channel Five show called *Cooking the Books* spoke to me. The conversation went a little bit like this...

'Lotte, we'd love you to come onto our show and compete against another chef with your own version of his recipe.' [*Oh, Lordy, never a good idea...*] 'No problem, would love to.' 'Excellent. So we thought we'd go with your take on Satay Chicken.' [*Erm... OK, nice and easy, but I do English country food, not entirely sure this makes sense...*] 'I'm sure I can do that for you.' 'Fabulous. The chef in question is Ken Hom.' [*What the..! Oh please no, he's the God of Chinese cooking...*] 'Absolutely fine [*so not fine! so not fine!*], this is so exciting [*absolutely terrifying*]. I've always wanted to meet him and I love his food.' 'OK, so could you get your version over to us by tomorrow and we'll go from there.' [*That is so ridiculously impossible right now; you would not believe how much work...*] 'Of course I can. It'll be tried and tested by then for you all and ready for the show' 'Thanks Lotte, you're a star. It's going to be a great show and I'm sure you'll give Ken Hom a run for his money.' [*Yes... whimper, whimper... whatever.*] 'A pleasure, yes I'll do my best!'

And I did do my best. And... lost. But then again I did get to cook with the great man and he thought my version quite yummy. And that was enough for me.

4 skinless free-range chicken breasts
2 eggs
1 small garlic clove, crushed
50g/2oz pumpkin seeds
50g/2oz pecan nuts
110g/4oz unsalted roasted peanuts (or buy salted, rinse in cold water and dry)
½ teaspoon ground cardamom seeds (split the pods with the back of a knife, remove the seeds, measure them and then crush with a pestle and mortar)
1 teaspoon ground ginger
1 teaspoon dried chilli flakes
½ teaspoon salt
Chilli jam (see below) and lime wedges, to serve

Cut the chicken into strips lengthways. Whisk the eggs in a bowl and add the garlic. Place the chicken in the egg and mix until all the chicken is well covered with the egg.

Combine the seeds, nuts, spices and rice flour into a food processor and pulse to combine, don't overprocess as you want the mixture to be crunchy. Pour it into a shallow dish.

Remove the chicken from the eggs and then dip into the nut mixture, making sure it is evenly and well coated.

Heat the oil in a frying pan and sauté the chicken four at a time until golden brown. Serve the chicken with Chilli jam and a squeeze or two of fresh lime juice.

chilli jam

This makes about 450g/1lb jam which is plenty for the chicken with some left over to go with cheese or cold meats. I often mix 1 tablespoon of jam with 4 tablespoons of mayonnaise and use this as a dip for sausage and chips – yum!

Makes 450g/1lb

2 large red chillies, sliced
450g/1lb ripe tomatoes, quartered
1 large onion, quartered
5 garlic clove
2 teaspoons chopped fresh ginger
1 tablespoon Thai fish sauce
225g/8oz demerara sugar
4 tablespoons cider vinegar
1 tablespoon balsamic vinegar

Put the chillies, tomatoes, onion, garlic, ginger and Thai sauce into a blender and whizz until it is just roughly chopped – don't overblend as you want a little texture to the jam.

Pour the mixture into a medium pan along with the sugar and vinegars. Bring to the boil and then reduce the heat and simmer for about 1–1½ hours. It can take a little while longer if you have particularly large and juicy tomatoes. You want the jam to be thick and syrupy, and the liquid on the surface should disappear. It will also look a bit darker. There may be some scum on the surface, but don't worry about this, as it will go when the chilli jam is cool.

Spoon the jam into hot sterilized (see page 83) jars.

The sealed jam will keep for a few months in a cool, dark place. Once opened, store in the fridge and eat within a month.

september

September used to bring the start of the school term, nowadays, later in the month it's university. What a change!

When Daisy went off for the first time I thought my heart would break. I wept uncontrollably as I drove off. I sobbed and blubbed and got rather snotty as I left my baby to fend for herself in the big bad world. I mourned my days that began and ended with her needs.
I longed for her wit and silliness. I even missed her occasional strops and hormone induced tempers.
Nowadays?

Well, nowadays, three years down the line, I pack Daisy off thinking how lovely it'll be to have a nice clean house...

...a home where trip hazards don't live on the stairs (what is it, that makes an able-bodied, intelligent girl incapable of removing things off the stairs and into her bedroom?).

An abode where plates don't get piled up on top of the dishwasher, but actually make it inside. A kitchen where there isn't a permanent pile of dirty clothes, that never goes down in size, and a sofa that isn't ravaged by over-use.

I think it'll be lovely; but realistically when she's gone back it's very quiet and a little boring. I love having her around. She's very funny, on occasion the mother in the relationship and just great, great company.

When I packed her off in the first year, I enclosed a little file with lots of my recipes. I piled a large box high with my old saucepans (years left in 'em!), raided Woollies for other kitchenalia, and hoped against hope that she would nourish herself sensibly and ingest the necessary vitamins and minerals to facilitate a first.

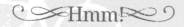

For those of you about to embark on the road to university and send your offspring into the arms of independence – please remember this:

You might have grand ideas about how you'd like your baby birds to feed themselves. It's possible you'll even be slightly smug as you think about the cookery lessons they attended before you dispatched them off...

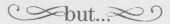

...in reality, their first year's diet will mostly be beer and chips with the occasional burger and kebab.

Second year is pretty much the same, although they might try a more varied diet that could include the odd chicken wing and Chinese takeaway. And perhaps, on occasion at three in the morning, there is the possibility that they'll stumble home with a curried number in their sweaty hands. This will soon be attached to their face and possibly a couple of hours later, down the loo. And worst of all, the next morning/afternoon, as they wake up from their cider-induced coma and turn over in bed, they'll re-visit the un-eaten goo attached to the pillow and the whole messy event will come flooding back.

Yes, the first and second years are a bit of a nutritional low point.

However, the third year should see some changes. By now, they'll be bored of trashy food, have made some seriously good friends and be living with them in one big house. They'll have grown up a bit and have mates over for meals. They'll try out some new dishes, and might even dig out the recipes you first sent them off with. There is even a small chance, that at some point, they'll read a cookery book.

Perhaps even this one!

So, in honour of beer and battered food – the following recipe is for all of Daisy's university friends:

thank you

for keeping her out of trouble, administering to her when she had flu, feeding her, making her laugh and taking her to A&E when she tripped over her handbag.

beer-battered alliums

I wrote this recipe for a TV show a few years back. I thought, instead of just onion rings, why not batter some of the allium family and then deep fry them. Please don't read this out of context – I don't usually go around administering GBH to innocent vegetables! I also like to use chive flowers – sometimes I still have a few of these in September if the weather has been mild. If not, don't worry, but, if you do make this in the height of summer, there will be plenty. Served with a quick-to-make dip they always disappear fast...!

For the garlic and chilli dip
6 tablespoons good-quality mayonnaise
1 red chilli, deseeded and finely
　chopped
grated zest of $^1/_2$ lemon
1 garlic cloves, crushed

For the batter
225g/8oz self-raising flour
2 tablespoons snipped fresh chives
$^1/_2$ teaspoon salt
1 large egg
425ml/15fl oz cold light beer (such as
　lager)
sunflower or groundnut oil, for frying

For the vegetables
2 bunches of spring onions, trimmed
　and halved lengthways
1 red onion, sliced thinly
1 white onion, sliced thinly
4 baby leeks, trimmed to leave just a
　little green, cut into four lengthways
chive flowers (optional)
sea salt, to serve

Combine all the ingredients for the dip and set aside until ready to serve.

Make the batter by sieving the flour into a medium mixing bowl. Add the chives and salt. Make a well in the centre and add the egg. Beat well, incorporating some of the flour. Now pour half the beer in, beat and then leave.

Fill a deep saucepan one-third full of oil. Heat the oil and check it is at the right temperature by dropping in a crust of bread – if it sizzles and browns the oil is ready.

Add the rest of the beer to the batter and beat.

Preheat the oven to 150°C/fan oven 130°C/gas mark 2. **Aga 4/3/2-door** *Simmering oven.*

Dip the alliums, a few at a time, in the batter and drop them gently into the hot oil. Only cook a few at a time, otherwise you'll bring down the heat of the oil and they'll become all soggy.

Drain on some kitchen paper, sprinkle with a little sea salt and keep warm in the oven until all the alliums are cooked. Serve with the chilli and garlic dip.

beetroot and goat's cheese salad with blackberry vinegar dressing

One autumn with a glut of blackberries and no wish to make any more jelly or jam, I decided to try making vinegar with them. It dresses this simple salad so very well.

8 rashers free-range dry cured, unsmoked streaky bacon
3 tablespoons olive or rapeseed oil
4 tablespoons Blackberry vinegar (opposite)
1 teaspoon wholegrain mustard
8 medium, cooked baby beetroot (not in vinegar)
2 tablespoons chopped fresh mint leaves
1 cos lettuce, leaves roughly broken up
110g/4oz soft, young goat's cheese.
salt and freshly ground black pepper

Preheat the grill to high. Place the bacon on a grill tray and cook, turning occasionally until it is crispy. Drain on kitchen paper and set aside.

AGA *Place the bacon on the small roasting tin rack. Now slide it onto the highest set of runners at the top of the roasting oven to grill. Turn occasionally until it is crispy. Drain on kitchen paper and set aside.*

Make the dressing by combining the oil, vinegar, mustard and a little seasoning together in a medium mixing bowl.

Cut each beetroot into four and add to the dressing, stirring to coat.

Combine the mint and lettuce leaves and divide them between four plates. Place the dressed beetroot quarters on top of the leaves. Break the goat's cheese up into little pieces and dot on top of the beetroot. Finish with two rashers of grilled bacon on top.

Blackberry vinegar

I often use this blackberry vinegar to dress hot baked beetroot. Mix it with a little crème fraîche and blob it over the top of them.

Makes approximately 570ml/1 pint

450g/1lb blackberries
570ml/1 pint white malt vinegar
450g/1lb caster sugar

Put the blackberries into a medium saucepan and mash them down with a fork. Add 1 tablespoon cold water and place over a gentle heat. Cover and simmer gently for 10 minutes.

Now transfer the berries to a medium mixing bowl and pour over the vinegar. Cover and leave in a cool place for 2 days, stirring occasionally.

After this time, strain the berries through a jelly bag or muslin cloth and leave to drip for an hour or so.

Place the juice and sugar in a medium pan and heat gently until the sugar dissolves. Bring to the boil and simmer gently for 10 minutes, removing any scum with a spoon.

Pour into sterilized bottles (see page 83) and keep in a cool, dark place for up to 1 year.

marrow stuffed with pork and beans and mustardy cheese sauce

I devised this recipe for a Gloria Hunniford show back in the late '90s. I think I may be one of those rare creatures that actually think a stuffed marrow isn't the work of the devil! It is simply perfect served with the Quick and easy cheesy mustard sauce, opposite.

Serves 4–6

2 marrows, each approximately
   900g/2lb
2 tablespoons olive oil
1 large onion, finely chopped
2 large garlic cloves, crushed
1/2 tablespoon chopped fresh sage
1 tablespoon chopped fresh parsley
1 English desert apple, peeled and diced
410g can cannellini beans, drained
225g/8oz minced pork
25g/1oz fresh white breadcrumbs
1 large egg, beaten
salt and freshly ground black pepper
Quick and easy cheesy mustard sauce
   (see below), baked potatoes or
   steamed broccoli, to serve

Preheat the oven to 180°C/fan oven 160°C/gas mark 4. **Aga 4/3-door** *Middle of baking oven.* **Aga 2-door** *Grid shelf on floor of roasting oven with cold plain shelf on second runners.*

Cut the marrows in half, lengthways and scoop out the seeds. Heat the olive oil in a medium, non-stick frying pan and fry the onion, garlic, sage and parsley gently together for 5 minutes. Add the apple and cook for a couple more minutes. Set aside to cool. Mix the beans, pork and breadcrumbs together in a large mixing bowl. Add the onion and apple mixture with the beaten egg and season with salt and pepper.

Tightly pack the meat into each halves of both marrows. Place the halves together again and tightly wrap each one in foil.

Place on a baking tray and cook for about 1 hour 15 minutes–1 hour 30 minutes. They are cooked when you can gently squeeze the marrow through the foil and it gives a little.

Unwrap and drain off any liquid. Slice the marrow and serve with the sauce. I like this with crispy baked potatoes and plenty of butter or for a lighter meal, some simply steamed broccoli.

Quick and easy cheesy mustard sauce

This is the all in-one method for making a cheese sauce. Perfect if you want to throw one together in a hurry.

Serve 4–6

50g/2oz butter
50g/2oz plain flour
570ml/1 pint semi-skimmed milk
225g/8oz mature Cheddar cheese,
   grated
50g/2oz Parmesan cheese, grated
2 tablespoons wholegrain mustard
1 tablespoons Dijon mustard
2 teaspoons English mustard
salt and freshly ground black pepper

Put the butter, flour and milk together into a medium, non-stick saucepan. Bring up to the boil, constantly whisking with a balloon whisk. Once at the boil, reduce the heat and simmer gently for 1 minute to cook the flour, still whisking all the time.

Now add the cheeses and mustards and season with the salt and pepper. Stir until the cheeses have melted and serve hot.

apple, blackberry and elderberry squidgy pudding

I can pinpoint the first time I smelt blackberries cooking. It was September 1976 and I'd gone out into the village lanes with my mum to pick them. We lived in a small Oxfordshire village called Great Haseley. A baker visited us twice a week and sold bread at the door. The local dairy farmer, John Smith, gave us milk, unpasteurised and fresh as a daisy, and a mobile bus shop, large, long and bright green parked up on a Wednesday and Saturday afternoon. My friend Sally and I regularly pinched the penny pink shrimp sweeties from there. (Which, if you are reading this, children, is very, very naughty!) Nothing, apart from the large bus, had really changed in Haseley for hundreds of years. I had my first lardy bread from our baker – it's a traditional bready cake made in Oxfordshire and Wiltshire. Nothing more than dough folded and twisted with currants, sugar and lard. Yes lard. Marvellous. The lard left a film on top of your mouth if you ate it cold – which I invariably did as I could never wait long enough for it to be warmed through, which I have to say is preferable. The blackberries we picked that day were specifically for jam. As my mum stirred them around the pan, with some apples from the garden, the kitchen was filled with a rich, fruity yet quite unusual smell – almost earthy. I'm not entirely sure the aroma of blackberries cooking is actually that wonderful – plums have a much better smell – but I loved it and have never changed that opinion.

Now, whenever I cook them, I don't feel I've moved house or even grown up. I'm still 10, with sticky, blackberry-stained fingers, blue teeth from eating too many and arms covered in thorn pricks. Nothing changes – I'm writing this having just been into the lane to pick some more for jelly – the blackberries had no desire to give up their fruit to me this evening – I had to fight for them. I'm scratched and bleeding with sticky blackberry stained fingers and blue teeth from eating too many! If you can't get hold of blackberries and elderberries for this delicious fruity treat, then replace them with some raspberries – frozen is fine. But if you do have a chance to plunder a hedgerow or two, you'll find they really do make this dish. I can honestly say this is one of my absolute favourite autumn puds.

Serves 4–6

450g/1lb dessert apples, peeled, cored
   and sliced
1 heaped tablespoon seedless
   raspberry jam
50g/2oz elderberries, de-stalked
110g/4oz blackberries
175g/6oz butter, softened
150g/5oz light brown muscovado sugar
1 tablespoon golden syrup
4 eggs, beaten
110g/4oz self-raising flour
110g/4oz ground almonds
1 teaspoon baking powder
$\frac{1}{2}$ teaspoon almond extract
cream or ice cream, to serve

Preheat the oven to 160°C/fan oven 140°C/gas mark 3. **Aga 4/3-door** *Grid shelf on floor of baking oven.* **Aga 2-door** *Grid shelf on floor of roasting oven with cold plain shelf on third runners.*

Put the apples, jam, elderberries and blackberries into a saucepan, cover and cook over a slow, gentle heat for 10–15 minutes or until soft. Spoon into a 1.1 litre/2 pint ovenproof dish.

Beat the butter, sugar and golden syrup together and gradually add the eggs, beating well between each addition. Fold in the flour, almonds, baking powder and almond extract.

Top the apple and raspberry mixture with the sponge mixture. Smooth the top and bake for 30–40 minutes until the sponge is golden brown and firm to the touch. If it does look a little brown on top before the middle is set, then cover with some foil and continue cooking.

Serve with a generous splodge of cream or ice cream.

roast lamb stuffed with cobnuts and courgettes

I'm always happy to let the wildlife in my garden eat half the blackberries, some of my soft summer fruit and work their way through the hundredweight of apples that tumble from my trees. I feel it's their right. However, I lose patience with my fluffy little friends when it comes to cobnuts and courgettes. I wait all year for the cobnuts, because they are so truly seasonal. Unlike imported, readily available nuts such as hazel or pine, autumn is the only time you can pluck them from our native trees, crack them and devour the creamy, buttery nut. Courgettes on the other hand, are available all year round. But I won't buy them. I tenderly plant the seeds, re-pot the seedlings and plant out the prickly plants so I can enjoy the flavour of a freshly picked courgette. It just cannot be compared to one that has travelled a fair few miles and hung around on a supermarket shelf for a few days. So imagine how I felt one day when Squirrel Nutkin and Peter ruddy Rabbit paid a visit! Just for a second, envisage my sad little face as I surveyed my vegetable patch and realised that the lovely yellow courgettes I was giving another day's growth to were now just stumps. The leaves and stalks; the engine room of the plants, were shredded, stripped and devoured. And can you visualize how heartbroken I must have been to see my poor nut tree with nothing on it. It was bare. Not one nut, a nutmeg or even a silver pear. I've only managed to make this lamb dish a few times, early in the season before the crazed fluffies come and do their worst. I must say though, the times I have been allowed to eat it, it was rather lovely.

Serves 8

For the stuffing
25g/1oz butter
1 onion, finely chopped
2 garlic cloves, crushed
1 medium courgette, approximately 110g/4oz, diced
$1/2$ tablespoon chopped fresh rosemary leaves
50g/2oz fresh white breadcrumbs
75g/3oz shelled cobnuts or hazelnuts, chopped (see Lotte's tips)
1 egg
salt and freshly ground black pepper

For the lamb
1.8kg/4lb leg of lamb, tunnel boned (ask your butcher to do this)
3 large onions, thinly sliced
275ml/10fl oz red wine
Baked sweet potatoes with leeks and cream (see page 75), to serve

Preheat the oven to 180°C/fan oven 160°C/gas mark 4. **Aga 4/3-door** *Middle of baking oven.* **Aga 2-door** *Grid shelf on floor of roasting oven with cold plain shelf on second runners.*

To make the stuffing, melt the butter in a medium, non-stick frying pan and add the onion, garlic, courgette and rosemary. Cook gently for 10 minutes. Leave it to cool for a couple of minutes.

Now add the breadcrumbs, cobnuts, egg and seasoning to the frying pan and stir well.

Spoon the stuffing inside the cavity of the lamb and secure with a skewer at each end or tie it with string. If you don't have either, just tuck the ends of the lamb underneath. The stuffing generally does try to make a run for it, but don't worry if it does, it'll all be eaten in the end!

Place the sliced onions in the bottom of a roasting tin and pop the lamb on top, pour 275ml/10fl oz cold water around it and lightly season with salt and pepper.

Roast in the oven, basting regularly, for $1^3/4$–2 hours depending on how pink you like your lamb. If you don't like it pink, then cook for a little longer. Once cooked, remove from the oven, cover and leave the joint to rest somewhere warm for 10 minutes, before you remove the string or the skewers. This gives the meat time to settle.

Now, skim off any fat from the onions left in the tin. Place the roasting tin on the hob over a medium heat and using a wooden spoon, scrape off the sediment and mix with the onions. Add the red wine and allow it to bubble until it has reduced by half. Taste and then season the gravy with salt and pepper.

Slice the lamb and serve it with the onions and the red wine gravy.

Lotte's tips
You can buy cobnuts in some supermarkets and greengrocers – but keep alert for squirrels lurking in the shadows – they will mug you for them with little thought of consequence!

baked sweet potatoes with leeks and cream

No calories in this at all. No butter, no cream, it's completely diet-friendly and won't attach itself to your thighs in anyway. OK, I'm fibbing. It's full of butter and cream, might attach itself to your thighs and there is an acute possibility that you'll put on a pound. But every creamy, sweet mouthful will be worth it. This is a delicious side dish to serve with the Roast lamb stuffed with cobnuts and courgettes (see opposite), but equally as yummy with any roasted meat and I have also served it with baked salmon.

Serves 4

25g/1oz butter
1 large leek, thinly sliced
700g/1½lb sweet potatoes, peeled and
    cut into 2.5cm/1 inch dice
570ml/1 pint double cream
freshly grated nutmeg
salt and freshly ground black pepper

Preheat the oven to 180°C/fan oven 160°C/gas mark 4. **Aga 4/3-door** *Middle of baking oven.* **Aga 2-door** *Grid shelf on floor of roasting oven with cold plain shelf on second runners*

Melt the butter in a large, non-stick frying pan and add the leek. Cook gently for 5 minutes or until soft.

Add the sweet potatoes and double cream to the pan. Grate over the nutmeg and season. Cook gently for 5 minutes then pour into a large ovenproof dish. Cover with foil and cook in the oven for 20 minutes. Remove the foil and continue to cook for a further 15–20 minutes or until the top is golden brown and the potatoes are soft.

plum and pistachio tart

The pudding is so easy to make. No effort at all. Just a bit of rolling, mixing and stoning of plums.

You see? Very little effort. So much so, it's probably a little bit cheeky to accept any compliments at all. But I insist you bask in your glory enormously when you serve it up because juicy plums adorning a pistachio frangipane is possibly the only way to eat them!

Serves 6–8

500g packet of puff pastry
75g/3oz unsalted, shelled, skinned pistachio nuts.
50g/2oz butter, softened
50g/2oz soft brown sugar
1 egg
450g/1lb ripe plums, stoned and halved
ice cream or clotted cream, to serve

Preheat the oven to 200°C/fan oven 180°C/gas mark 6. **Aga 4/3/2-door** *Grid shelf on floor of roasting oven.*

Roll out the puff pastry to a rectangle measuring 35x25cm/14x10 inch. Lay it on a baking sheet and with the back of a knife, score the pastry 2.5cm/1 inch from the edge, all the way around in a straight line. Prick the pastry in the centre with a fork to prevent it rising during cooking. Chill in the fridge.

Whizz the pistachios in a food processor until they are finely chopped.

Place the butter and sugar in a medium mixing bowl and cream them together. Stir in the egg and nuts.

Spread the nut mixture over the base of pastry, taking it up to the scored line near the edges. Lay the plum halves, skin side up, closely together over the nut mixture.

Bake for 25–35 minutes or until the pastry and fruit are cooked.

Serve with ice cream or clotted cream!

warm green tomato relish

This relish is lovely on the side of hot roast lamb or the next day in a sarnie with the cold meat and some salad leaves. Come late September, I always have quite a few green tomatoes that the sun has quite frankly given up ripening. This is a great way to use them up. Again, this is an instant chutney, so although you can eat it straight away, it doesn't last as long.

Serves 6–8

25g/1oz butter
1 medium onion, thinly sliced
3 garlic cloves, crushed
700g/1½lb green tomatoes, chopped
1½ tablespoons light brown
    muscovado sugar
2 tablespoons balsamic vinegar
a little extra light brown muscovado
    sugar and balsamic vinegar
salt and freshly ground black pepper

Melt the butter in a large saucepan over a medium heat and add the onion and garlic. Cover and sweat gently for 10 minutes.

Add the tomatoes and sugar and cook until soft, about 10 minutes.

Now add the vinegar and seasoning. Taste and add a little more of the sugar and vinegar to your taste and serve warm.

If you are not using the relish straight away, transfer it to a lidded plastic container and store in the fridge for up to 10 days. Heat through gently before serving.

sweetcorn and clam chowder

In mid to late September the sweetcorn that I grow are just a little too tough for munching from the cob. Earlier in the summer, I pluck them straight from the plant and place them into the pot to steam. They need no more than a few minutes to cook. I then plunge them into some cold salty butter and eat them standing up in the kitchen, tea towel around my neck and butter dripping off my chin. The sweetness is almost unbearable and I am a little wild eyed as I sink my teeth into the compliant kernels. I feel like an addict. The flavour and act of eating fresh sweetcorn is too intense for words and I have to do it on my own. I can't share the experience. Besides, it's a little embarrassing as I make too many groaning and moaning sounds.

But come September, I eat my corn in a different way. With clams, in a spicy chowder. Steam the sweetcorn until tender and then, when they are cool enough to handle, stand them upright on a board, hold with one hand and with the other, cut the kernels off from top to bottom with a sharp knife. You can do this with the uncooked cobs, but I prefer to cut when they have been steamed – it's a little easier. For this recipe, you need the kernels from about 4–6 cobs, depending on their size. Or use canned sweetcorn – which I can happily eat on its own and out of the can with a spoon. I have been known to do the same with baked beans!

25g/1oz butter
110g/4oz unsmoked streaky bacon, cut into 2.5cm/1 inch pieces
1 large onion, chopped
1 large red pepper, chopped
1 small red chilli, deseeded and finely chopped
1 teaspoon garam masala
2 medium potatoes, peeled and evenly diced
570ml/1 pint vegetable stock
25g/1oz plain flour
570ml/1 pint full-fat milk
275g/10oz sweetcorn, fresh, frozen or canned
280g can clams, drained
2 tablespoons chopped fresh parsley
salt and freshly ground black pepper
crusty bloomer, to serve

Heat the butter in a large saucepan and add the bacon. Let it sizzle gently until it starts to colour. Now add the onion, pepper and chilli. Cook gently for 5 minutes.

Sprinkle the garam masala into the pan, stir and cook for 1 minute. Toss in the potatoes, pour in the stock and bring to the boil. Simmer until the potatoes are tender, but not falling apart, about 10 minutes. Remove the pan from the heat.

Whisk the flour and 150ml/$\frac{1}{4}$ pint of the milk together, until there are no lumps, and add to the soup. Stir until boiling, simmer for a minute and then add the rest of the milk.

Now pour in the sweetcorn and stir in the clams. Taste and season. Don't overdo it with the salt as the clams have been soaked in brine.

Simmer for a couple of minutes, add the parsley and then serve with the crusty bread.

lamb pasties

I do love a pasty. It does everything it promises. It doesn't lie, fool around or break your heart. A pasty nourishes you, fills you, comforts and cuddles you from the inside out. It doesn't need a frilly garnish or a poncey sauce to make it more attractive. It's simple, loving, and at times when you might need it most – your very best friend.

The incredible soured cream pastry makes another entry into the book (it's also used in the Jamakewell tart on page 34) in this recipe. I truly believe it is one of the easiest pastries in the world. Why it isn't the first one anyone ever makes, I don't know. Shortcrust is a tough nut to crack and not very easy, so why on earth do they teach it to beginners? If everyone made soured cream pastry first, it would give them the confidence to try other pastries. It rarely goes wrong, has a wonderful texture, is easy to roll out and when cooked, is light, buttery and very similar in texture to flaky or puff pastry. Serve these little friends with nothing more complicated than a dressed ripe tomato salad with a sprinkling of chives and a glass of cold cider.

Makes 4 large pasties

For the pastry
175g/6oz plain flour
150g/5oz unsalted butter, cubed and
    chilled
7 tablespoons soured cream
flour, for dusting
1 egg, beaten

For the filling
25g/1oz butter
1 large onion, thinly sliced
1 tablespoon maple syrup
450g/1lb minced lamb
1 large sweet potato, peeled and cut
    into 5mm/¼ inch dice
1 tablespoon chopped fresh parsley
1 sprig fresh rosemary
salt and freshly ground black pepper
tomato salad, to serve

Preheat the oven to 200°C/fan oven 180°C/gas mark 6. **Aga 4/3/2-door** *Grid shelf on floor of roasting oven*

To make the pastry, place the flour in food processor with the chilled and cubed butter. Whizz the flour and butter together until it resembles breadcrumbs. Add the soured cream and whizz again until the pastry just starts to come together. Turn the mixture out onto a floured worksurface and gently knead it together until a dough is formed. Chill for 1 hour.

For the filling, melt the butter in a small frying pan over a gentle heat, add the maple syrup and the sliced onion. Stir well and cook gently for 15 minutes.

Place the cooked onion, lamb, potato and parsley in a large mixing bowl. Add 2 tablespoons water and season with the salt and pepper. Stir well to combine.

Divide the pastry into 4 equal pieces. Dust a worksurface with flour and roll out each piece to form a circle approximately 20cm/8 inches in diameter. Cut the pastry out using a plate - it doesn't have to be bang on 20cm/8in!

Spoon the lamb and vegetable mixture into the centre of each pastry circle and then place a couple of rosemary leaves on top. Brush around the edges with some water and then bring the sides up over the filling and crimp the edges to seal.

Place the pasties on baking sheets and brush them with beaten egg. Chill for 15 minutes.

Bake in the oven for 35-40 minutes. If they look a little too brown after 25 minutes loosely cover with some foil and continue to cook.

Serve the pasties with a tomato salad and a glass of cider.

plum vodka or gin

Actually I think I might be wrong about juicy plums adorning a pistachio frangipane being the only way to eat them (see Plum and pistachio tart page 150). Plums steeped in vodka or gin is possibly the only way to drink them.

Makes approximately 1 litre/ 1³/₄ pints

450g/1lb plums
110g/4oz caster sugar
1 litre/1³/₄ pints vodka or gin

Place the plums and the caster sugar together with 4 tablespoons cold water into a medium saucepan. Place over a gentle heat and cook until the sugar has dissolved and the plums are tender. Cool.

Pour the vodka or gin over the plums and stir. Transfer to a couple of wide mouthed 1 litre/1³/₄ pint Kilner jars, secure the lids in place and set aside to steep in a cool, dark place for 2 months.

Strain (reserving the plums, see Lotte's tips) and then bottle and drink. It's lovely with tonic and a slice of lime or just neat.

Lotte's tips
The alcohol-soaked plums will keep for up to 3 months and are delicious in Christmas pudding or cake...! Or I occasionally put one or two in a pie.

Sloe gin
Purist sloe gin makers might seek me out for a telling off when they read what I'm about to say. However my method for making sloe gin has served me and my friends and family terribly well (!) over the years.

Most people will tell you that you should only pick the sloe berries after the first frost because this makes the skin burst and in turn will give a better colour and flavour to the gin. I would agree with that on the flavour and colour front, but I just can't be bothered to seek out a frost before I pick the sloes.

The other thing they may say is that each and every sloe gin berry must be individually pricked with a darning needle to release the flavour and break the skin. Who's got time for that?

Sloe picking, as romantic as it can be on a misty autumn morning, has to fit in with everything else I do. So, I pick them and... bung them in the freezer overnight. Who needs Jack Frost when you can do this?

To make the gin, first you need to pick approximately 450g/1lb sloes and freeze them. Once they are frozen, pop them into a demijohn bottle. Pour 1 litre/1³/₄ pint gin and 6–8 heaped tablespoons caster sugar on top of the sloes, if you want it a bit sweeter by all means add a little more. Then set aside for an hour or so to let the berries defrost.

When the berries have defrosted, give the bottle a good shake, the skins will split (no darning needle required!) and your sloe gin with eventually be a lovely dark pink with tons of flavour. Agitate the gin every few days to start with, then every week, then every month. I leave mine to steep for at least a year; I've even been known to leave it for two.

After this time, strain through muslin and re-bottle. It's fabulous with tonic or delicious with cheese at the end of a meal.

winter tonic jelly

I really wish I'd come up with the name of this jelly myself. It's slightly annoying. It was made and jarred and was awaiting labels before being put onto the shelf that doubles up as my shop where I sell jellies and jams on my demonstration days. I couldn't think what to call this heavily spiced jelly which contained different fruits brimming with vitamin C. I imagined how yummy the jelly would be on toast and scones. I knew how soothing it would be as a hot drink for a winter cold. Two teaspoonfuls in a cup, some boiling water – ta da! But what should I call it? 'I think Winter tonic jelly is the answer Lotte' said my friends Pete and Sue (not quite together, but nearly in sync). Brilliant! And damn. The amount this recipe makes will vary according to how much fruit you use and how big your pan is!

approximately 900g/2lb windfall apples, quartered (don't peel or core them)
approximately 900g/2lb mixed autumn fruit, eg blackberries, elderberries, damsons, plums or blackcurrants
juice of 2 lemons
3 star anise
12 cloves
2 cinnamon sticks
granulated sugar (the quantity will depend on how much juice you get)
a small piece of muslin and some string

Place the fruit in a large saucepan or preserving pan. Add the lemon juice and enough cold water to cover the fruit.

Bring the fruit and water to the boil and simmer for 30–40 minutes or until the fruit is soft and pulpy. I put mine in the simmering oven of the Aga all day, stirring it occasionally to prevent the top drying out.

Allow the fruit to cool for about 10 minutes then transfer it to a jelly bag and let it drip through overnight. Don't push it through the bag as you'll make the jelly cloudy – just let it do its own thing.

The next day, measure the liquid into a large clean saucepan or preserving pan and for every 570ml/1 pint of juice add 450g/1lb sugar. Wrap the star anise, cloves and cinnamon sticks in the muslin, tie with string and add to the pan.

Heat the juice gently until the sugar dissolves and then bring it up to the boil. Simmer the jelly until it reaches setting point (see Lotte's tips). Remove the spices, pour the jelly into sterilized jam jars (see page 83), seal and label.

The jelly will keep in a cool, dark, dry place for up to 1 year.

Lotte's tips
To tell if the jelly has reached setting point, use a sugar thermometer (it will show the setting point for jelly, usually 105°C) or drip some jelly onto a plate straight from the freezer. If the jelly wrinkles on the plate when you put the end of a teaspoon through it, it's at setting point.

Another wonderful addition to this jelly is a sloe berry. But not just any sloe – no, these are the sloes that I've steeped in the gin for a year or two. When I finally get around to straining my homemade sloe gin, I add the sloe berries to my jelly at the initial cooking stage, and mash them down with all the other fruit. It really does add quite a zing to the jelly and goes beautifully with the spices. I hate to see good food go to waste and even though they've done their job with the gin, they still have something else to offer and that is to make this Winter tonic jelly just a bit naughty.

october

Oooh, I do love a bonfire.

I've started cutting back the garden now, and the pile of twigs, leaves and mess is getting ever larger. It's time to bring out my trusty, rusty old incinerator.

As I burn the summer away, I always start thinking about warm soups, comfort food and the dark afternoons to come.

These cold nights and chilly mornings are welcome after the dry days of summer and, as I stoke the fire, I can't help but get excited at the prospect of stew and a dumpling... or two.

I adore Ireland. I've had some of the best times of my life there.

Everyone has a great capacity for fun and the Irish surely must have the most generous nature of any country.

And, even though I've since found out my great grandfather was a Cork man, I only went there for the first time, in a very warm October six years ago to film with the BBC. I travelled with Martin the producer/director/camera/sound (there is a lot of multi-tasking in TV nowadays!) and Fanny, who was second camera/researcher then – now she is Head of Food in a large TV production company.

Our first port of call was Margaret and Michael Browne's house. Margaret, or The Duchess of Cork, as I like to call her is now one of my dearest friends and my collaborator in various silly evenings.

In fact the first night there, I discovered poteen in the middle of filming, their wine cellar by 8pm and their infamous warm whiskeys by midnight.

'Just one more small one Lotte?'
'Yeah, that would be lovely.'

'Just one more small one Lotte? Go on, it's good for you, it will help you sleep.'
'OK, just one more then I really have to go to bed.'

'Just one more small one Lotte?'
'One more, then that is it.'

'Just one more small one Lotte?'
[Slurring] *'I have to bed the stairs and up sleep teeth paste.'*

I left them all, including 93 year-old Kitty (mother of Duchess) downstairs as I stumbled to bed. Kitty was still at it 'til 4 in the morning.

If you are ever in Ireland, and offered 'just one more small one' may I offer a free piece of advice? Say yes – they are delicious! However, be prepared to do nothing the next day.

Since then, Duchess and I have stayed at each other's houses a lot. I have to go to Cork at least once or twice a year to get my fix and every time I seem to come back in a terrible state. Only recently, Daisy picked me up at Birmingham Airport limping through the gate looking very worse for wear – all because after a few gin and tonics I thought I was the lead in Riverdance!

In The Duchess' defence, it wasn't her fault. She wasn't even there. I had spent the day with Maureen her sister-in-law. I'd been taken under her wing – along with her husband Dickie.

'Lotte, just one small one at the pub? Dickie is there with my son and some friends.' (Oh, Lordy, I knew where this was going.)

'Would love to Maureen, sounds a fabulous idea, but just one small gin and tonic.'

I love Irish pubs – all the men talk to you. Maureen's son was there with some friends, including Kieran who took a bit of a shine to me. I'm not sure whether it was my glowing personality or the fact that his friends had told him that I owned a twelve million euro house in Dublin, (which I don't!) but he fell reasonably hard and proceeded to sing Irish love songs to me.

'Just one more small one Lotte?
'Ok, one more.'

Twelve small ones later, when the live music started I got up and under the hazy influence of good Irish humour thought I could do a jig.

Apparently I can't. My Achilles tendon strapped up with a large tubigrip and 2 aspirins told me I really, really can't.

Still, I had Kieran at my feet, so it wasn't that bad. His name is Kieran Leachy (pronounced Leakey). I did have to break it to him gently that I couldn't possibly marry him. If I did, my name would be Lotte Leachy – and that is what I do when I sneeze or laugh too much.

leek and pear irish rabbit

My friend Jennie and I went to Cork once and on returning she said, 'Lotte I can see why you feel so at home there. They're all as bonkers as you!' So true. The English and Welsh have their rabbit/rarebit – it's essentially posh cheese on toast. Now, I've given the Irish their own version, made with soda bread. I've also added pear and leek – because I can – well I am the author. Ireland has, in my opinion the best smoked salmon in the world, and I think it goes beautifully with the pear and leek. Obviously you don't need to go to Ireland to retrieve the salmon, but why not? Have a small one for me!

Serves 2

4 slices soda bread (preferably the
   lovely Kitty's, see page 164)
25g/1oz butter
1 small leek, sliced
1 large ripe pear, peeled, cored and
   diced
1 teaspoon dried sage
200g/7oz Cheddar cheese, grated
2 egg yolks
1 teaspoon English Mustard
4 tablespoons cider
110g/4oz smoked salmon (optional
freshly ground black pepper

Lightly toast both sides of the soda bread.

Melt the butter over a medium heat in a medium non-stick frying pan, add the leek and soften for 5 minutes. Add the pear and sage and cook for a few minutes until the pear is soft. Set aside.

Put the cheese, egg yolks, mustard and cider in a small saucepan and stir over a gentle heat until you get a lovely thick creamy mixture. Don't boil though; otherwise you'll get scrambled eggs. Season with a little black pepper.

Preheat the grill to high.

Place the toast on a baking sheet, lay the smoked salmon, if using, on top of the toast. Divide the leek and pear mixture on top of this and then pour over the thick cheese sauce.

Cook under the hot grill until bubbling and brown and serve immediately.
Aga 4/3/2-door *Grill at the top of the roasting oven.*

Kitty's brown soda bread

Kitty was Margaret's mother and a fabulous cook. She passed the recipe for her famous soda bread onto her daughter and Margaret published it in her very own cookbook, *Through My Kitchen Window*. I eat Kitty's soda bread every morning at Margaret's when I visit. She is the most amazing cook, which is why we were filming with her in the first place. Whenever I'm in Cork I eat like a queen, which is very fitting considering I'm dining with The Duchess!

Makes one 20cm/8-inch round loaf

butter, for greasing
275g/10oz plain white flour
175g/6oz wholemeal flour
1 tablespoon oatmeal or bran
1 teaspoon bicarbonate soda
1 teaspoon cream of tartar
435ml/15fl oz buttermilk
salt

Preheat the oven to 220°C/fan oven 200°C/gas mark 7. Place a baking sheet in the oven to heat. **Aga 4/3/2-door** *Lower roasting oven, place a baking sheet in to heat.*

Grease a 20cm/8-inch non-stick cake tin.

Mix the flours, oatmeal or bran, bicarbonate of soda, cream of tartar and a pinch of salt together in a mixing bowl. Incorporate as much air as possible. Make a well in the centre and pour in the milk.

Draw in the mixture from the sides with a wooden spoon, and mix gently in a full circular movement until a soft, moist dough is formed.

Knead the dough gently and put it in the cake tin, pressing it out to fill the tin. Cut a cross shape into the top of the bread. Place the tin on the preheated baking sheet and cook for 20 minutes.

Then reduce the heat to 180°C/160°C fan oven/gas mark 4 for a further 20 minutes or until the bread is cooked. **Aga 4/3-door** *Middle of baking oven.* **Aga 2-door** *Grid shelf on floor of roasting oven with cold plain shelf on second runners.*

Test by turning out and tapping the bottom of the bread with your fingers. If it sounds hollow then it is cooked. Cool on a wire rack.

The soda bread will keep for 2–3 days in an airtight container in a cool place.

mackerel, caper and gherkin fishcakes with homemade horseradish mayonnaise

I've made these fishcakes with fresh mackerel, fresh and smoked and smoked and canned – and every version tastes great. We have quite snobby ideas about canned fish in this country, and we shouldn't. The fish is caught and canned fresh, therefore the taste is delicious, and we all know that oily fish is packed full of all those omega thingys that we're forever being told to eat more of. I always have a stack of canned fish in my cupboard to snack on, put into salads or turn into fishcakes.

Horseradish is something I love. Fresh is divine (a bit of a bully in your garden, so be careful where you plant it) and one sniff of just-grated horseradish is sinus-clearing to a degree. When making roast beef I add it to the gravy and I also love it next to a kipper! It's an unlikely but wonderful partner to fish and it elevates these fishcakes to superior status!

Serves 4

3 x 125g cans mackerel fillets in
   sunflower oil, drained
225g/8oz cold cooked new potatoes in
   their skins
2 tablespoons chopped gherkins
2 tablespoons capers in brine, drained
   and chopped
1small red onion, finely chopped
1 heaped tablespoon chopped fresh
   parsley
1 heaped tablespoon snipped fresh chives
75g/3oz rolled oats or finely ground
   oatmeal
2 eggs, beaten

4 tablespoons sunflower oil, for frying
salt and freshly ground black pepper
Homemade horseradish mayonnaise
   and buttered peas, to serve

Place the mackerel and potato in a medium mixing bowl and roughly mash them together with a fork – don't be tempted to use a food processor as it will make the mixture glutinous and mushy.

Stir in the gherkins, capers, onion, parsley and chives. Season with black pepper.

Divide the mixture into 8 and shape into flat, round cakes. Pop them on a plate, cover with clingfilm and leave in the fridge for at least a couple of hours or overnight to firm up.

If you are using rolled oats whizz them in a food processor until they are fine.

Tip the beaten eggs onto a large flat plate and spread out the oats or oatmeal on another. Dip the fishcakes in the egg, covering well and then into the oats. It is really important that you make sure the sides are well covered.

When you are ready to cook the fishcakes, preheat the oven to 150°C/fan oven 130°C/gas mark 2.
AGA 4/3/2-door *Simmering oven.*

Heat a shallow film of oil in a large, non-stick frying pan over a medium heat. Add the fishcakes, in batches of 4 and fry for 6 minutes or so on each side until they are golden brown and hot all the way through. Keep the fishcakes warm in the oven while you cook the remainder.

Drain on kitchen paper and serve with a good dollop of Homemade horseradish mayonnaise and buttered peas.

Homemade horseradish mayonnaise

2 egg yolks
275ml/10fl oz sunflower oil
1 tablespoon cider vinegar
1 tablespoon chopped fresh parsley
$^{1}/_{2}$–1 tablespoon horseradish sauce (see
   Lotte's tips)
salt and freshly ground black pepper

Put the egg yolks into a bowl with a narrow base. Add a pinch of salt and pepper. Whisk the egg yolks with an electric beater. As you are whisking, gradually add the oil, slowly, from a jug, drop by drop to start with and then, when you've used up half the oil, in a thin stream until it is all used up.

If the mixture gets too thick, dilute it with a little of the vinegar as you go along. This will loosen the mix and make it easier to absorb the oil. After you have added all the oil add any remaining vinegar and stir well.

Season with a little more salt and pepper and then add the parsley and the horseradish to taste.

Lotte's tips
If you can get hold of some fresh horseradish, use this instead. Grate enough of it into the mayonnaise until you like the taste. It is much hotter, so be careful!

lamb with damsons and rosemary dumplings

This dish was my mother's nemesis. I often bought it along to her parties, as an extra dish to help out. It was the first to go. Everyone swarmed towards it and devoured it in its entirety. She smiled a pained smile whenever anyone inquired as to how she made it. Could she possibly give them the recipe? Oops. I'm lucky enough to have damsons in my garden, but if you don't and you haven't got a friend you can pilfer some from, use plums – they are just as delicious. I've even made this dish with greengages before, and apricots work well too.

Serves 6

For the stew
2 tablespoons rapeseed oil
900g/2lb leg of lamb, diced and fat trimmed off
25g/1oz butter
12 baby onions, peeled (see Lotte's tips)
4 large carrots, cut into 2.5cm/1 inch chunks
3 parsnips, cored and cut into 2.5cm/ 1 inch chunks
1 tablespoon soft brown sugar
2 tablespoons plain flour
275ml/10fl oz red wine
570ml/1 pint lamb or beef stock
1 tablespoon chopped fresh parsley
1/2 teaspoon dried thyme
1 fresh bay leaf
1 sprig of fresh rosemary
350g/12oz damsons, plums. greengages or apricots, halved and stoned
salt and freshly ground black pepper

For the dumplings
225g/8oz self-raising flour
150g/5oz suet
1 heaped tablespoon chopped fresh rosemary leaves
mashed sweet potato, to serve

Preheat the oven to 180°C/fan oven 160°C/gas mark 4. **Aga 4/3-door** *Middle of baking oven.* **Aga 2-door** *Grid shelf on floor of roasting oven with cold plain shelf on second runners.*

Heat a flameproof casserole dish over a medium heat and pour in the rapeseed oil. When it starts to smoke, start browning the meat. Only add a few pieces at a time as too much meat in the pan at any one time will bring down the temperature, and start to release the water in the meat. This will start to stew the meat and not brown it. You want the stew to be a lovely deep brown so you seal and caramelise the meat and this gives the whole stew a richer colour. When each batch of meat is sufficiently browned, remove and set aside.

Melt the butter and add the onions, carrots and parsnips to the pan and fry gently for about 5 minutes over a low heat until they are just coloured. Add the brown sugar at this stage as it helps the process of browning and gives a lovely sweet taste to the dish. Keep the temperature gentle as you don't want to burn the sugar.

Now stir the flour into the vegetables and cook it for a couple of minutes. Add the red wine and leave it to bubble away for a couple more minutes. Pour in the stock and bring to boiling point, replace the meat and add the herbs. Make sure the bay leaf is split to release the flavour and tucked underneath the lamb with the rosemary.

Cook in the oven for 1 1/2 hours until the lamb is tender. Remove, stir in the damsons and taste and season with salt and pepper. Increase the oven temperature to 200°C/180°C fan oven/gas mark 6. **Aga 4/3/2-door** *Grid shelf on the floor of the roasting oven.*

Now make the dumplings, these must be made and cooked straightaway because as soon as you add water to the raising agent in the flour it starts to work. If you make and leave the dumplings aside for a period of time before cooking, they will be lumpen and heavy. Never let an uncooked dumpling hang around! Sieve the flour into a medium mixing bowl and add the suet and rosemary. Season with salt and pepper. Add 150ml/5fl oz cold water and stir to form a pliable dough. If you make the dumplings too dry, they'll be heavy and hard. It's better to have the mixture on the wetter side. Roll the dumplings into golf ball-size balls and place them on top of the lamb. Pop back into the oven uncovered to let the dumplings cook for 10 minutes.

Remove the dish from the oven, turn the dumplings over and cook for a further 10 minutes until golden brown.

Serve the stew and dumplings with some mashed sweet potato – it goes beautifully!

Lotte's tips
I find the easiest way to peel baby onions, is to place them in a bowl and pour boiling water over them. Leave the onions until they are cool and then peel them, keeping the root intact.

autumn chicken pie

I tested this recipe for the first time on the Slipper Shufflers (see Doddie's Almond and chocolate meringue!). It was declared delicious, yummy and divine – probably the wine talking. You don't have to cook a chicken especially for this recipe – I often use the leftover chicken from a Sunday roast for this pie on a Monday. Pick the rest of the meat off and make a stock with the bones as below. This pie is positively brimming with autumn colour. It's cheap to make, filling and one of my absolute favourite dishes.

Serves 6–8

For the chicken
1kg 350g/3lb free-range chicken
1 carrot, cut into chunks
1 onion, quartered
2 celery sticks, sliced
1 fresh bay leaf
a sprig of fresh thyme
a sprig of fresh parsley
6 black peppercorns

For the pie
50g/2oz butter
1 large leek, thinly sliced
2 red peppers, thinly sliced
225g/8oz mushrooms, quartered
1 small butternut squash, peeled and
    evenly diced (see Lotte's tips)
1 teaspoon dried thyme
5 tablespoons plain flour
$^{1}/_{2}$ tablespoon wholegrain mustard
2 tablespoons Dijon mustard
flour, for dusting
500g packet of ready-made puff pastry
1 egg, beaten
salt and freshly ground black pepper

To cook the chicken, place it in a large saucepan and cover it with cold water (about 1.7 litres/3 pints) and add the carrot, onion, celery, herbs and peppercorns. Bring to the boil, and simmer for 1$^{1}/_{2}$ hours or until the meat is falling off the bones. **Aga 4/3/2-door** *Place in the simmering oven.*

Set the cooked chicken aside until it is cool enough to handle. Remove all the meat from the chicken, put the leftover bones back into the stock and then simmer for another 30 minutes. Strain the stock through a sieve into a clean pan and discard the bones and vegetables.

Preheat the oven to 200°C/fan oven 180°C/gas mark 6. **Aga 4/3/2-door** *Grid shelf on floor of roasting oven.*

Cut the chicken meat into bite-size pieces and place it in a 2.3 litre/4 pint pie dish.

Reduce the chicken stock in the pan over a high heat until you have 850ml/1$^{1}/_{2}$ pints in volume.

Melt the butter in a large, non-stick frying pan or saucepan and fry the leek and peppers for 5 minutes over a gentle heat. Add the mushrooms, diced squash and thyme and cook for a couple of minutes.

Blend the flour into the vegetables and slowly add the reduced stock, stirring all the time. When it has thickened, simmer for 2 minutes; add the mustards and season with salt and pepper. Spoon over the chicken, stir well and allow to cool down.

Now, dust a worksurface with flour and roll out the pastry to the right size and shape to top the dish. Cut a long, thin strip of pastry long enough to go around the rim of the dish. Dampen the edges of the dish and place the strip around the edge. Cover the pie with the pastry and decorate with any cut-off pieces. Knock up the edges of the pastry, crimp and glaze with the beaten egg.

Place the pie on a baking sheet and cook in the oven 30 minutes.

Reduce the oven temperature to 160°C/ fan oven 140°C/gas mark 3 and cook for a further 30 minutes. **Aga 4/3-door** *Grid shelf on floor of baking oven.* **Aga 2-door** *Grid shelf on floor of roasting oven with cold plain shelf of third runners. If it gets too brown, loosely cover with a little foil to protect the pastry.*

Lotte's tips
When choosing a butternut squash, pick one with a fat neck and a smaller rounded bottom. This is because most of the flesh is in the neck and the seeds are in the rounded bit. If you buy one with a large bottom (!) it will be mainly seeds.

I do love a glass (or two!) of rosé wine – last year Sue and I contributed and kept buoyant, the rosé wine sales in the south of France for a few days in October.

I do believe they are still eternally grateful to us, what with a recession and all that! Tom and Liz who live next door to me and opposite Sue, kindly loaned us their apartment in La Napoule and we planned a girl's week away from kids, work and responsibilities. We planned trips to Marseille by train, ambles through Cannes, Nice and a visit or two, to a castle or vineyard. In reality none of this happened. For we discovered a little restaurant on the beach called Le Spot and its *pichets de rosé*!

Our mornings were usually spent buying some bread and cheese, a couple of pastries and the days supply of anchovy-stuffed olives. This was followed by a page or two of our books and the inevitable snooze on the beach. Our internal alarm clocks usually aroused us at 11.30am and we shuffled along to Le Spot. *'Pichet de rosé s'il vous plaît.'* Delicious. *'Another,* (for I can't speak French very well) *pichet de rosé s'il vous plaît.'* I love that the French didn't bat an eyelid at our second bottle before midday. It was to them, quite normal. I would have a very large *Tuna Niçoise*; Sue had a *Croque Madame* (that'll be a *Croque Monsieur* with a large fried egg on top). After lunch, we'd shuffle back to our little patch of sand and – you've guessed it – fall into a warm, sunny, deep and restful, rosé-induced sleep. Just marvellous.

Our alarm clocks would sound again at about 5pm, after perhaps turning over and basting once or twice and it was time to have a coffee to perk us up. Six o'clock found us back in the apartment for showers and the rosé/anchovy/olive ritual.

On our small travels to the local shops (for we never made it out of La Napoule until the day we left) we bought and tried out a few different local rosés. A cheap three-euro bottle was our favourite – no idea of its name, it was the shape of the bottle that attracted us, which was all curvy. After curvy rosé and a jar of olives, it was time to find somewhere to eat. There were lots of lovely local places, which late in the season you didn't have to queue for.

Our favourite was Dumbo's. Not its real name, but one I am ashamed to admit I came up with because the lovely lady who ran it, had very big ears. On our initial visit there, we were so hungry that we lost all manners. When approached by the owner (I now can't call her Dumbo, it's so mean – let's say her name was Madame X) we were found to be sucking the mayonnaise out of the sachets. Thankfully she laughed and perhaps filed it away as another strange thing the English do, then topped up our supply. And every time we ate there, Madame X would do the same, it was our canapé when spread over the warm bread.

The rosé wasn't particularly nice at Madame X's, and on our last night, with this in mind, we decided to have a couple of bottles before we went there. As we both ever so slightly fell into the restaurant, in anticipation of the mayonnaise, I noticed a family to my right. Suddenly the daughter piped up, in a broad Birmingham accent, *'Aren't yow that laaady who cooks on the talee?'* Oh, Lordy. *'Yow were sitting behind ous on the plaaane.'* What are the chances of that? Well, Sue did most of the talking as I had somewhat lost the power of speech to the rosé. As it turns out this really lovely family **were** sitting behind us on the plane and in the time they'd spent in La Napoule, they **had** travelled out and seen a whole world of wonderful things. Sue and I, shattered from lots of work and under the evil spell of rosé, hadn't. Shame on us. Next time...?

Anyway... the point of all this preamble is: if you too have a love of something pink that comes in a curvy bottle – and you don't manage to drink it all – use it for this fabulous dish.

annie's rosé chicken

Years ago, I was sitting in Annie's kitchen one afternoon and she told me she had friends for supper that night, and needed inspiration. I had a look in her fridge and saw chicken, rosé wine, orange, tarragon and crème fraîche. I jotted down a quick recipe for her and the rest is history...

Serves 4

25g/1oz butter
1 medium onion, finely chopped
4 large skinless, boneless chicken
   breasts
2 tablespoons chopped fresh tarragon
grated zest and juice of 1 medium
   orange
150ml/5fl oz rosé wine
300ml crème fraîche
salt and freshly ground black pepper
fresh tarragon, to garnish
Pea and mint mash (see page 90) or
   boiled rice, to serve

Melt the butter in a large, non-stick sauté pan and add the onion. Cook it gently for 5 minutes over a low heat, but don't allow it to brown.

Now add the chicken breasts and sprinkle over the chopped tarragon. Scatter over the orange zest and pour in the juice and wine. Bring up to the boil and then reduce to a simmer. Simmer on the hob for 30 minutes, with the lid half on, or until the chicken is cooked through and firm. **Aga 4/3/2-door** *Cook in the simmering oven.*

Remove the chicken from the pan using a slotted spoon, place on a plate and cover with foil. Put the pan back on the stove and bring to the boil for 1 minute. Add the crème fraîche and stir. Return the chicken to the pan and season.

Serve garnished with fresh tarragon. I think this is delicious with my Pea and Mint mash or just some simply boiled rice.

You are probably wondering who on earth Annie is? Well, many years ago in the days when I did gym classes, and when Daisy was small I met up with a bunch of lovely girls at the local gym. We all had little children and when we weren't looning around in trainers and luminous thonged leotards (that era should never have been allowed, it was very wrong), we drank a lot of coffee and spent an awful lot of time together. As a collective noun, we called ourselves The Slappers – I would hope in an ironic way! We still meet up some 18 years later, and I could happily write a book about our various lives – a lot has gone on. I love The Slappers and do wish I could see them more, but life just gets so busy and it's very easy to not make a dinner until catch up. So, Annie is a slapper.

doddie's almond and chocolate meringue

I have another very old friend called Doddie. A peculiar name you'll agree, and a name invented by Daisy when she was 18 months old. Doddie and I had a catering company together when Daisy was little and she used to follow Doddie around everywhere calling her Dowa. (That was pretty odd in itself!) Because I thought it was funny, and because I often look for an excuse to be utterly ridiculous, I thought it would be terribly witty to call her Doddie Dowa – this was Daisy's word for dog! Looking back, it's not really that funny, but at the time I wept with laughter as Doddie just threw me one of her withering looks. Doddie and I went to Winkfield Place in Windsor when we were 17 – to learn how to cook Cordon Bleu. And that's how we met. Well, learning to cook was one option – the other apparently was to find a husband. We were regularly shipped off to Sandhurst military academy to Scottish dance with the officers and I was often flung around by some militant and very mean army boy to the 'Dashing white sergeant'. Apparently how many bruises you could inflict on a Winkfield girl was a running bet – I believe they won hundreds of pounds on me.

Another couple of birds we met there are Sian and Gilly. We still get together on occasion for a glorious food-filled, wine-flowing night in. As a collective, we call ourselves the Slipper Shufflers (and after a glass or two, this is often pronounced the Shipper Slufflers). This is because the next morning, shuffling in our slippers is the only thing we are capable of! The great thing about Doddie, apart from the fact that she is a wonderful friend – is her ability to have me completely convulsed with laughter with just one look; one flick of an expression, one twitch of the mouth. I believe she is the only person in the world who can do that to me – and on many occasion, it's got us both into lots of trouble.

And another of Doddie's amazing talents is her mind-blowing ability to consume chocolate and puddings. I've seen her inhale tubes of Smarties, bury her face in trifle, and dive head first into the odd chocolate roulade or two. But the most irritating quality of all? She doesn't put any weight on. Not a bleeding ounce. Doddie – this pudding is for you. Hope you get fat!

Serves 6–8

butter, for greasing
flour, for dusting
175g/6oz ground almonds
5 egg whites
275g/10oz caster sugar
1 teaspoon vanilla extract
½ teaspoon malt vinegar
275ml/10fl oz double cream, lightly
    whipped
175g/6oz good-quality dark chocolate
1 tablespoon icing sugar
2 tablespoons dark rum
icing sugar and grated chocolate,
    to decorate

Preheat the oven to 200°C/180°C fan oven/gas mark 6. **Aga 4/3/2-door** *Grid shelf on the floor of roasting oven.*

Butter and dust with flour, 2x20cm/8-inch sandwich tins. Line the bottom of each tin with a disc of baking parchment.

Spread the ground almonds on a baking tray and toast them in the oven. Check them at 1 minute intervals, stirring them around so they brown evenly. They can burn very easily, so keep a close eye on them. Browning usually takes about 2–3 minutes.

Reduce the oven temperature to 180°C/fan 160°C/gas mark 4.

Place the egg whites in a large mixing bowl and whisk them until they are very stiff. Gradually whisk in the sugar, 1 tablespoon at a time. Continue whisking until the egg whites become very stiff again, and then add the vanilla extract and the vinegar.

Gently fold in the almonds and spoon the meringue into each baking tin, dividing it equally. Smooth over the tops and bake for about 15–20 minutes or until the meringue is firm. **Aga 4/3-door** *Middle of baking oven.* **Aga 2-door** *Grid shelf on floor of roasting oven with cold plain shelf on second runners.*

Remove from the oven and leave to cool for 5 minutes in the tins. Turn the meringues out onto a wire rack and remove the discs of baking parchment.

Whilst the meringue is cooling, place the chocolate in a heatproof bowl over a pan of just simmering water and melt the chocolate with 2 tablespoons of water and the icing sugar. Stir until it is a thick, creamy consistency. Leave to cool.

Fold the cooled chocolate mixture into the whipped cream.

Choose the nicest meringue half for the top of the cake. Place the other one on a serving plate, drizzle over the rum and spread the chocolate cream all over. Pop the remaining meringue on top and then dust with icing sugar and sprinkle the grated chocolate over. Pop the meringue into the fridge for an hour to allow the chocolate cream to set and then serve.

november

I declare November to be Pie Season.

Asparagus get their own season, so do strawberries and game shoots. So why shouldn't the humble pie, a dish that has its roots steeped in British history, not have its own season too?

From now on, I have decided that November will be pie time, pie month, pie moment... pie SEASON! We are all going to embrace the pie, devour the pie, demolish the pie and... er... eat it... a lot. Or else...!

beef and smoked oyster pie

I used to make a smoked oyster butter to melt onto chargrilled steaks. Delicious as it was, it wasn't actually my idea, just a recipe I inherited with my first job. I ran the kitchen of a local wine bar when I was just out of college. It was a nutty time, and the weekends were always fun – especially when the local rugby boys were in. I do believe I managed to fit them all in my old Mini once and gave them a lift home. It was a little cramped and cosy, but immensely enjoyable! I do love a rugby player. I think this particular pie would appeal to them actually. All rugged pastry with manly, meaty filling. Chunky thighs – oops sorry – vegetables and a rich, dark, muscular sauce; seasoned with the earthy, scrum(my) flavour of smoked oysters. With this pie, I believe I might catch those lovely boys – Hooker, Wing and Centre! Ooh, I feel a little flushed, and over-excited. I've gone all unnecessary. Time for a lie down I think!

Serves 6–8

For the pie filling
4 tablespoons plain flour
900g/2lb beef stewing steak, diced into 2.5cm/1 inch pieces
3 tablespoons rapeseed oil
25g/1oz butter
2 large onions, chopped
4 large carrots, peeled and cut into chunks
275g/10oz button mushrooms, quartered
1/2 teaspoon dried thyme
275ml/10fl oz beef stock
275ml/10fl oz red wine
1 tablespoon anchovy essence
1 tablespoon mushroom ketchup
85g can smoked oysters in sunflower oil, drained and sliced (see Lotte's tips)
salt and freshly ground black pepper

For the suetcrust pastry (see Lotte's tips)
275g/10oz self-raising flour
1/2 teaspoon salt
1 teaspoon dried thyme
3 teaspoons English mustard powder
150g/5oz shredded suet
flour, for dusting
1 egg, beaten
buttered green cabbage, to serve

Preheat the oven to 160°C/fan oven 140°C/gas mark 3. **Aga 4/3-door** *Grid shelf on floor of baking oven.* **Aga 2-door** *Grid shelf on floor of roasting oven with cold plain shelf on third runners.*

To make the filling, place the flour into a medium mixing bowl, season with the salt and pepper and toss in the meat. Remove to a plate, shaking any excess flour off.

Heat the oil in a large flameproof casserole dish and fry the beef in small batches until browned on all sides. Remove and set aside.

Now melt the butter in the dish and gently fry the onion for 5 minutes until soft and then add the carrots, mushrooms and thyme. Cook for a further 5 minutes.

Add the stock, wine, anchovy essence and mushroom ketchup. Replace the meat and bring to the boil, reduce to a simmer and cook gently in the oven for 1 1/2 hours.

After this time, add the oysters, taste and adjust the seasoning and then spoon the filling into a 1.7 litre/3 pint pie dish.

Increase the oven temperature up to 190°C/fan oven 170°C/gas mark 5. **Aga 4/3-door** *Top of baking oven.* **Aga 2-door** *Grid shelf on floor of roasting oven.*

Make the pastry just before you need it because just like dumplings, when you add a liquid to self-raising flour it starts the rising process and you need to cook it straight away to keep the pastry light. If you leave the pastry hanging around, it will be heavy and tough. Sieve the flour into a medium mixing bowl and add the salt, thyme and mustard powder. Stir in the suet and mix in 175–200ml/6–7fl oz cold water to form a soft dough. Turn onto a floured board and knead until smooth.

Now roll out the pastry, large enough to cover the pie dish with a little overhang. Moisten the rim of the dish with some water and position the pastry on top and press it over the edge of the dish, and tuck it slightly under. It doesn't matter if the edges are thick and pleated, this is a very rustic pie and the rougher the better!

Make a slit in the centre of the pastry to let the steam escape and brush all over with the beaten egg to give a rich colour to the cooked pastry. Stand the pie on a baking sheet and bake in the oven at for about 45–60 minutes until the pastry is crisp and golden brown.

Slice the pie and serve with buttered green cabbage.

Lotte's tips
The smoked oysters, although unusual really do give this pie a wonderful smoky depth of flavour. Don't avoid putting them in. I'm not fond of a fresh oyster, but I love these smoked ones and can eat them straight from the tin.

This suetcrust pastry is comfort food at its very best. Crispy and believe it or not, quite light, it adorns a pie beautifully and reminds you that home-cooking on a wintry day is the best reason of all to light a fire, close the curtains and feast with friends and family.

chicken and anchovy trust-me-pie

The smoked oysters don't make the Beef and smoked oyster pie (see page 176) fishy, they just add an intense seasoning. The anchovies in this recipe do the same thing. I realise I'm asking you to trust me on this, and I'm also aware that anchovies are the work of the devil for so many. But honestly if you can get past a bit of anchovy prejudice, you'll see that this pie does work – it's quite fantastic.

Serves 4–6

3 large, boneless, skinless free-range
    chicken breasts
grated zest and juice of $1/2$ lemon
$1/2$ teaspoon dried thyme
1 tablespoon rapeseed oil
50g/2oz butter
1 large leek, thinly sliced
225g/8oz mushrooms, roughly chopped
250ml full-fat crème fraîche
50g can anchovies in sunflower oil,
    drained
1 tablespoon wholegrain mustard
flour, for dusting
500g packet of ready-made puff pastry
1 egg, beaten
freshly ground black pepper
steamed broccoli, peas and carrots,
    to serve

Preheat the oven to 200°C/fan oven 180°C/gas mark 6. **Aga 4/3/2-door** *Grid shelf on floor of roasting oven.*

Cut each chicken breast into thin strips, place in a dish, and pour over the lemon juice and sprinkle over the zest and thyme. Leave to marinate for 30 minutes.

Heat a large non-stick frying pan, add the rapeseed oil and fry the chicken strips for about 5–6 minutes on either side until they are thoroughly cooked all the way through. Remove and cool.

Now, melt the butter in the frying pan and add the leeks and mushrooms. Cook gently for 10 minutes or until the leeks are tender. Add the crème fraîche and cook for 1 minute. Season with some black pepper. Transfer to a plate and spread the mixture out to allow it to cool quickly.

Drain the anchovies, roughly chop them and place them in a small bowl. Add the mustard and mix well. Season with a little black pepper.

Dust a worksurface with flour, roll out two-thirds of the pastry and use it to line a 25cm/10-inch springform cake tin, leaving about a 2.5cm/1 inch overhang. Spread the anchovy and mustard mixture all over the bottom of the pastry.

Put half the chicken fillets on top of the anchovy mixture. Cover with half the leek and mushroom mixture. Spoon the other half of the chicken on top and finish with a final mushroom layer.

Roll out the remaining pastry to fit on the top of the pie. Lay it over the top and then bring the overhang of pastry into the centre to meet it. Crimp and fold the edges over to make it all snug. Brush the pastry with beaten egg. Transfer onto a baking tray and chill for an hour or so or overnight if you want.

Bake the pie for 35–40 minutes or until the pastry is golden brown and the inside is piping hot. Use a long knife to test how hot it is – gently pop it into the middle of the pie, leave it in for 15 seconds, pull it out and if the knife is hot, so is the filling! It may take a little longer to cook, to ensure the filling is hot, if the pie has been in the fridge for a while. If this is the case, cover it with foil after the 35–40 minutes and continue to cook until the filling is piping hot.

Slice and serve the pie with steamed broccoli, peas and carrots.

homemade Oxford sausages with spiced red cabbage

These homemade sausages are so simple to make and are cooked in the oven with the cabbage – easy! Oxford sausages are traditionally patty-shaped and are unusually, skinless too so there's no faffing about involved with casings. I think the smell of spiced red cabbage gently simmering away in the oven is one of the most beautiful aromas a kitchen can offer. This is such a perfect autumn dish with the deep, rich colours matching all the crinkly leaves that spend October on my grass – I'm terrible for not raking! This is also the month I stop my relentless jelly production, and leave the final windfall apples to rot. Not so good for the grass, but delicious for the flocks of Fieldfares that feast on them throughout the winter.

Serves 8

For the cabbage
butter, for greasing
1 large red cabbage, approx 900g/2lb, thinly sliced
450g/1lb red onions, thinly sliced
50g/2oz butter
175g/6oz pitted prunes, halved
2 large dessert apples, peeled, cored and sliced
grated zest and juice of 1 large orange
2 tablespoons cider vinegar
2 heaped tablespoons dark brown muscovado sugar
1/2 teaspoon ground cloves
1 teaspoon ground cinnamon
1 teaspoon ground ginger
salt and freshly ground black pepper

For the sausages
900g/2lb minced pork
225g/8oz fresh white breadcrumbs
grated zest of 1 small lemon
1/2 teaspoon grated nutmeg
2 teaspoons dried thyme
2 eggs, lightly beaten
2 tablespoons rapeseed oil
mashed potato or Saffron mash (see page 197), to serve

Preheat the oven to 160°C/fan oven 140°C/gas mark 3. **Aga 4/3-door** *Grid shelf on floor of baking oven.* **Aga 2-door** *Grid shelf on floor of roasting oven with cold plain shelf on third runners.*

Grease a large flameproof casserole dish with butter. Lay half the cabbage in the bottom of the dish. Put half the onions on top with 25g/1oz of the butter and then the prunes and apples. Sprinkle over the orange zest and juice, then the vinegar and sugar. Now add all the spices and season with salt and pepper.

Cover with the remaining onions and cabbage and then dot over the rest of the butter. Cook in the oven for 1 1/2 hours.

To make the sausages, place the pork, breadcrumbs, lemon rind, nutmeg, thyme and egg in a medium mixing bowl. Stir together to combine and season well with salt and pepper.

Divide the mixture into 8 equal portions and shape it into 7.5–10cm/3–4-inch round patties. Set aside in the fridge to chill for 30 minutes.

Pour the oil into a large, non-stick frying pan over a medium heat and cook the sausages for 4 minutes on each side. Transfer to a plate.

After the cabbage has been cooking for 1 1/2 hours, remove it from the oven, stir to mix it up and take half of it out. Pop the sausages in amongst the cabbage and then replace the cabbage back on top. Return it to the oven for 30 minutes.

Serve this with some lovely fluffy mashed potato, perhaps the saffron one from December – perfect fodder for a chilly November day.

lamb pie with pear and cranberry

The idea of fruit and meat is very English, very old and very delicious. We initially got the idea from our spice trade with the Middle East, but we ran with it over the years, and came up with some lovely recipes of our own. When I first wrote this one, I did think it might be a step to far. However, after a bit of testing and tweaking I managed to get the right balance of sweet, sour, fruit and meat. You actually don't have to make this into a pie; it could just be a simple stew with a jacket potato or my favourite – fluffy mash.

Serves 6–8

For the pie filling
1–2 tablespoons rapeseed oil
900g/2lb leg of lamb, diced and
    trimmed of fat
25g/1oz butter
1 large onion, roughly chopped
3 large carrots, cut into 2.5cm/1 inch
    chunks
1 tablespoon soft brown sugar
2½ tablespoons plain flour
570m/1 pint lamb or beef stock
150ml/5fl oz red wine
2 tablespoons chopped fresh parsley
½ teaspoon dried thyme
1 fresh bay leaf
a small sprig of rosemary
2 large pears, peeled, cored and cut
    into chunks the same size as the
    lamb
110g/4oz fresh cranberries
grated zest and juice of 1 small orange
½ tablespoon clear honey or quince
jelly
1 tablespoon chopped fresh mint
salt and freshly ground black pepper

For the suetcrust pastry
225g/8oz self-raising flour
2 teaspoons dried thyme
2 teaspoons of English mustard powder
110g/4oz shredded suet
flour, for dusting
1 egg, beaten
steamed runner beans, to serve

Preheat the oven to 160°C/fan oven 140°C.gas mark 3. **Aga 4/3-door** *Grid shelf on floor of baking oven* **Aga 2-door** *Grid shelf on floor of roasting oven with cold plain shelf on third runners.*

Heat 1 tablespoon of the oil in a large flameproof casserole dish and brown the pieces of lamb a few at a time. When each piece of meat is sufficiently browned, remove it using a slotted spoon and transfer to a plate. You might need to add another tablespoon of oil to brown all the meat.

Now add the butter, onion, carrots and brown sugar to the dish and fry them gently until they are beginning to soften and then caramelise due to the sugar. You don't want the sugar to burn, so keep the heat low. It just makes the vegetables sweeter and gives a lovely colour to the final dish.

Stir in the flour and pour over the stock and wine. Bring up to boiling point, return the lamb to the dish with the parsley, thyme, bay leaf and rosemary. Season with a little salt and pepper.

Cook in the oven for 45 minutes Remove and then add the pears, cranberries and orange zest and juice. Cook for another 15 minutes. Taste and adjust the seasoning. Add the honey or quince jelly.

Now pour into 1.4 litre/2½ pint pie dish and set aside to cool a little.

Increase the oven temperature to 190°C/fan oven 170°C/gas mark 5. **Aga 4/3-door** *Top of baking oven.* **Aga 2-door** *Grid shelf on floor of roasting oven.*

Make the pastry just before you need it because just like dumplings, when you add a liquid to self-raising flour it starts the rising process and you need to cook it straight away to keep the pastry light. If you leave the pastry hanging around, it will be heavy and tough. Sieve the flour into a medium mixing bowl and add the thyme, mustard powder and a pinch of salt. Stir in the suet and mix with approximately 150ml/5fl oz cold water to make a soft dough. Turn onto a floured board and knead until smooth.

Now roll out the pastry, big enough to cover your pie dish with a little overhang. Moisten the rim of the dish with some water and position the pastry on top and press it over the edge of the dish, and tuck it slightly under. It doesn't matter if the edges are thick and pleated, this is a very rustic pie and the rougher the better!

Make a slit in the middle to let the steam escape during cooking and brush all over with the beaten egg to give a rich colour to the cooked pastry. Stand the pie on a baking sheet and bake in the oven for about 45–60 minutes until the pastry is crisp and golden brown.

Slice the pie and serve with steamed runner beans, tossed in butter and plenty of seasoning.

~Christmas is coming...

Who would have thought that this solid, fruit packed, spicy pudding started its life as a fragrant pottage? Like so many British dishes, it has evolved over the centuries from a simple peasant's meal to a subtlety of celebration. A pottage was a soup prepared with cheap cuts of meat, grains, breadcrumbs and vegetables. Over Yuletide it was eaten with the addition of expensive spices, such as cinnamon and nutmeg – these gave it its celebratory touch. The liquid content was reduced over the years and in the early 17th century, it was boiled in a muslin cloth and began to look like the spherical pudding we see on our Christmas cards today. Over the next couple of centuries the meat disappeared altogether and the only remaining token of meat left in the pudding now, is the suet.

The Sunday before advent is known as Stir up Sunday. Advent is the month before Christmas and the time of preparation prior to the birth of Christ. We now associate this Sunday as the time to make your Christmas pudding because the prayer that is said on this particular day begins with the line 'Stir up we beseech thee' (the real essence of this prayer is the organisation and preparation for the coming of Christ). Stir up Sunday is now our reminder to hurry home and make the Christmas pudding. It needs to be made on this day, so it has a month to mature and

Christmas pudding really does benefit from this maturing. The flavour of the spices mellow and deepen, the fruits plump up and soften, and if you are like me and enjoy feeding the pudding with copious amounts of rum, you'll find that it does indeed taste superb. A pudding that has been allowed to mature for a whole year is even better – so make two now and have one ready for next year!

When you have gathered all your ingredients, and as you are creating this delicious concoction, get each member of your family to take a turn at stirring the mixture. As they do, they can each make a wish. This is an old tradition and one I do every year with Daisy. Another tradition is to place an old sixpence in the pudding. Nowadays I use a pound, (big enough to find and small enough not to be a nuisance) and I also wrap it in a piece of greaseproof paper. This is the best way to ensure Auntie Doris doesn't choke! There are various explanations surrounding the sixpence and other trinkets that are combined into the pudding. If you do find the coin you are going to die rich, a thimble indicates that you may never be married and if you discover a ring, prepare yourself, you will be married within the year. No cheating now, only one ring per pudding! ~

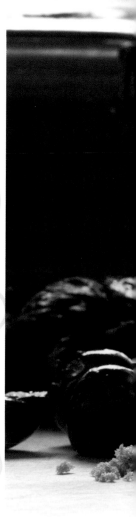

my christmas pudding

You've no idea of the personal sacrifice I've made over the years to bring you the perfect Christmas pud.

I've tested and tasted many puddings, written and cooked dozens of recipes and eaten my way through pudding after pudding, just to give you my very best recipe. At times I'll have you know, I've even resembled one in shape and...um... texture.

All for you. So, I think you'd better go ahead and make this... now! Go on... chop, chop, get yourselves off to the shops and start steaming. It is, quite frankly the least you can do!

Serves 8–10

butter, for greasing
175g/6oz seedless raisins
50g/2oz currants
75g/3oz sultanas
110g/4oz dried pear, roughly chopped
110g/4oz dried figs, roughly chopped
50g/2oz glacé cherries, halved
finely grated zest of 1 lemon
finely grated zest of 1 orange
1 large cooking apple, peeled, cored and grated
110g/4oz fresh white breadcrumbs
1 tablespoon plain flour
1 teaspoon ground mixed spice
$\frac{1}{2}$ teaspoon ground ginger
$\frac{1}{4}$ teaspoon salt
110g/4oz shredded suet
75g/3oz soft light brown muscovado sugar
1 tablespoon golden syrup
2 large eggs
4 tablespoons dark rum
4 tablespoons cherry brandy
1 tablespoon semi-skimmed milk
£1 coin, rinsed with boiling water, wrapped tightly in greaseproof paper
holly, to decorate
rum, rum butter, Sherry sauce (see page 41) or custard, to serve

Lightly grease a 1.2 litre/2 pint pudding basin and line the base with baking parchment.

Put the raisins, currants and sultanas in a large mixing bowl with the dried pear, figs, cherries, lemon and orange zest, grated apple, breadcrumbs, flour, mixed spice, ginger, salt, suet, sugar and golden syrup. Stir to mix.

Place the eggs, rum, cherry brandy and milk in a jug and whisk them together. Add the liquid to the fruit mixture and stir well. At this stage add the greaseproof-wrapped pound and let the family take turns to stir the pudding and make a wish.

Spoon the mixture into the prepared pudding basin and press it down well. Cover the surface with a disc of greaseproof paper. Take a piece of foil and a piece of greaseproof paper, both big enough to cover the bowl, with enough overhang to secure with string. Make a pleat in the centre of the foil and the greaseproof (to allow for expansion during steaming) and place on top of the bowl. Secure the foil and paper tightly in place with string.

Conventional hob Place the pudding basin into a large saucepan and pour in enough boiling water to come halfway up the basin. Now bring the water up to the boil, cover the pan and boil steadily for 8 hours, topping up with boiling water if necessary to ensure the saucepan doesn't boil dry.

Aga *Put the Christmas pudding into a large pan and pour in enough boiling water to come halfway up the basin. Cover, bring to the boil and then simmer on the simmering plate for 30 minutes. Top up with some more boiling water and then transfer the pan to the simmering oven for 12 hours or overnight.*

Once cooked, remove the pudding from the pan and allow it to cool completely. Then re-cover with some fresh greaseproof paper and foil. Store the cooked pudding in a cool, dark place for at least 4 weeks.

To reheat on Christmas day
Conventional hob Steam the pudding for 2 hours as above and then turn out onto a warmed serving dish.

Aga *Put the pudding in a large saucepan and pour boiling water half way up the sides. Cover, bring up to the boil and simmer on the simmering plate for 30 minutes, then transfer to the simmering oven for 2 hours.*

To serve, warm some rum in a pan, and set it alight with a match. Pour this over the pudding and decorate with the holly. Serve with rum butter, Sherry sauce (page 41) or an enormous amount of custard!

bread pudding

Forgive me, for I am about to say something a bit naughty. Serve this pudding with some ready-made canned custard. You know, the one that comes from that county next to Cornwall. My cousins, Richard and Andrew, and I were weaned on it! We like it so much we drink it from the jug. One Christmas, Richard even put a table fire out with it. Bit of a long story – it involved a candle, a cracker joke, the fortune telling fish, a pink paper hat, lead piping and Colonel Mustard.

Serves 1

butter, for greasing
225g/8oz white bread, preferably stale
425ml/15fl oz semi-skimmed milk
225g/8oz mixed dried fruit eg raisins,
    currants, sultanas and dried apricots
75g/3oz soft brown sugar
50g/2oz butter, softened
2 teaspoons mixed spice
2 large eggs, beaten
$\frac{1}{2}$ teaspoon ground nutmeg
demerara sugar, to sprinkle
canned custard or Vanilla and bay
    custard sauce (see page 17), to serve

Preheat the oven to 180°C/fan oven 160°C/gas mark 4. **Aga 4/3-door** *Middle of baking oven.* **Aga 2-door** *Grid shelf on the floor of roasting oven with cold plain shelf on second runners.*

Grease an 18cm/7-inch square tin with butter.

Break the bread into small pieces and place in a large mixing bowl. Pour the milk over the bread and leave it to soak for 30 minutes.

Then mix the bread and milk together with a fork to form a smooth, squidgy mixture. Add the fruit, sugar, butter, mixed spice and beaten egg and mix well.

Pour the mixture into the greased tin, smooth the top with the back of a metal spoon and sprinkle with nutmeg. Bake for about 1–1$\frac{1}{2}$ hours until firm and browned.

Allow the pudding to cool a little in the tin before cutting it into squares. Sprinkle the pudding with demerara sugar and serve with hot canned custard and nothing else! Or if you're really not keen on canned custard try it with Vanilla and bay custard sauce (see page 17).

december

Forget the diet gurus, their healthy eating plans and their advice about how to be sensible during this silly season of food, wine and all that is abundant and naughty. This is a most wonderful time of year: when friends and family gather at your home to laugh, eat, drink and be very merry. A time of total indulgence, frivolity and fun. It doesn't have to be too much work and it doesn't have to be expensive. All it should be is a time of cheeriness, happy faces and very fully tummies... with perhaps a dram... or three... of something warming!

Remember: 'tis the season to be 'very' jolly!

Every year I hold 'Easy Christmas entertaining' and 'Preparing ahead for Christmas' demonstrations. These, along with the summer ones in my garden, are the most popular.

Why?

Because Christmas brings with it a hefty amount of terror at just how much work is involved in enjoying yourself. People want to know how to 'get through' and not necessarily how to 'enjoy' this lovely time.

It seems such a shame. It really shouldn't be that hard to cook a roast dinner and a pudding. Most families do it every Sunday without too many disasters. So why does the thought of feeding Christmas lunch to family and friends bring with it so many nightmares?

I don't think my type help. We spend an awful lot of time putting the pressure on and coming up with complicated versions of the roast turkey. We throw in new and not terribly exciting ways to cook your Brussels. (I confess to stir-frying them with beetroot one year on the BBC. Sorry.) And we extol the virtues of new pans to change your life and special thermometers to shove up and check the temperature of your turkey's bottom. (Sorry again.)

So, the following recipes of mine are to give you an easy Christmas. There are dishes you can cook ahead of time and freeze. Recipes that are perfect to eat on the days around the 25th. I've given you my Pork rebellion recipe – which I served up last year for Christmas, and possibly made it my easiest ever (by the way pork rebellion isn't a new fancy cut!).

Yes, I too get a little wired and frazzled over those few days. I'm human and the pressure on me to perform is just as hard. I'm not stupid though – I delegate. Everyone has a job, be it peeling, stuffing or pouring me a large glass of wine. Don't let others get away with sitting down and watching TV while you are stuck, sweating and attacking the turkey alone in the kitchen. There is no point in being a martyr. Look what happed to Joan of Arc – burnt on a stake for her trouble.

Just enjoy Christmas. Prepare ahead with my recipes. Stick some in the freezer and make a few the day before. Don't worry if you are late serving the food; stick two fingers up to the grumblers! It's your day too to enjoy, so do what is easiest – for you.

Or if in doubt – break open a bottle of cheap fizz, pour in some peach juice with a squeeze of lime and call it breakfast – works for me.

boozy mincemeat

This mincemeat is a bit of a triumph. I make it every year without fail and sell most of it off at my cookery demonstrations and use the rest to feed everyone over Christmas. What I love the most is that there is absolutely no suet in it so it's not greasy. It is literally just preserved with sugar and booze – hence the terribly original title. Realistically it needs about two weeks to mature, but I have used it after a couple of days and it's still lovely. So make some at the beginning of the month and by the time you start to bake with it, it'll be scrumptious.

Makes 4 x 450g/1lb or 8 x 225g/ 8oz jars

1 large dessert apple, peeled, cored and grated
1 tablespoon lemon juice
110g/4oz no-soak, dried apricots, roughly chopped
110g/4oz dried pears, roughly chopped
110g/4oz dried figs, roughly chopped
110g/4oz dried dates, roughly chopped
110g/4oz glacé cherries, roughly chopped
juice and grated zest of 1 large orange
225g/8oz sultanas
225g/8oz raisins
4 tablespoons orange marmalade
175g/6oz soft brown sugar
175g/6oz demerara sugar
3 teaspoons ground mixed spice
$\frac{1}{2}$ teaspoon freshly grated nutmeg
150ml/5fl oz dark rum
150ml/5fl oz brandy

Toss the grated apple in the lemon juice. Place all the ingredients in a large bowl and stir until mixed well.

Cover the bowl and leave to steep for 2 days, stirring occasionally until the fruit has all plumped up and absorbed the booze, sugar and spices.

Then pot in sterilized jars (see page 83), cover and store in a cool place.

Lotte's tips
Once you've made the mincemeat, you can use it for the following recipes in this chapter Mulled cider (see opposite), Mince pies with orange and almond pastry (page 194) and Apple and mincemeat frangipane tart with sour cream pastry (page 199).

mulled cider

Mulled wine is not my favourite drink. It has the annoying habit of turning your mouth purple. This is quite embarrassing at a party, where you are trying to make a particularly intellectual point, or say something witty. I remember making a mental note not to drink the red at my mum's funeral when I saw Doddie. There was this indigo plimsoll line of wine around the edge of her lips and her teeth had turned a dark shade of crimson. There followed a fairly conscious decision to stick to the brandy. Doddie had sworn, that because she was my very lovely friend, that she wouldn't leave the wake until I had – to support me. She did manage to stay upright until I left, but was later put to bed by her husband, fully dressed and singing smutty rugby songs. The next morning she phoned me to see if I was alright. Apparently the red wine hadn't been a terribly good idea – she told me that as she drove past the crematorium on her way to work in Oxford that day, it had taken all her self-control not to drive in and beg them to take her there and then. Only Doddie could say that to me the day after I had cremated my mum – I laughed so much, I thought I'd be sick! I know my mother would have thought it very funny too. Anyway, mulled cider is the way to go. It doesn't stain your teeth and is the perfect drink to offer your friends at a Christmas party. It also has the added benefit of making your house smell lovely and Christmassy when people arrive.

Makes 2 litres/3$^{1}/_{2}$ pints

2 litres/3$^{1}/_{2}$ pints medium sweet cider
3 tablespoons Boozy mincemeat
(see opposite)
2 dessert apples, sliced
1 orange, sliced
1 fresh bay leaf
10 whole cloves
1 cinnamon stick
3 tablespoons dark brown muscovado
sugar

Heat up all the ingredients together in a large saucepan. Do not bring to the boil – just a gentle heat.

Leave for 1 hour for the flavours to infuse and then reheat to just below boiling and serve.

Lotte's tips
If there is any Mulled cider leftover, strain and re-bottle it. Keep in the fridge for up to 10 days for any unexpected guests. You can either just reheat it without the fruit for a quick drink, or add a few orange slices and another spoonful of the mincemeat.

mince pies with orange and almond pastry

I just love a mince pie. Daisy and I have them while we put the Christmas tree up. I insist on Christmas songs, a glass of Baileys on ice and a mince pie, then I really know it's Christmas. We struggle to bring the tree in together, stand it up (luckily, John the chap I always buy the tree from in Thame attaches a special wooden stand for me). I usually have to cut the top off because I always buy one too tall, and inevitably we have a small bicker as Daisy gets bored, gives up halfway through and falls asleep on the sofa. I'm usually left to finish and then put up the rest of the decorations. Does this happen to everyone else too? I only drink Baileys at this time of year – or perhaps when we have a snowy day in the lane. We all live at the bottom of a steep hill and too much snow means no work and no school. A couple of years ago, on an incredibly snowy morning, we all met for a monumental snowball fight and toboggan race down the hill. Soaked and freezing, everyone came to my cottage where we cooked bacon and egg sandwiches, hot chocolate for the children and coffee with a slug of Baileys (instead of milk) for the big people. As the snow came down, we drank a little more and as it started to melt we settled down in front of the fire and had a lovely afternoon snooze. We all spend a lot of our time in the lane hoping for snow. Make these pies in advance and then freeze them. Take them out as you need them and warm them through in a low oven. Quite wonderful on their own or with a splodge of clotted cream.

Makes 12 (see Lotte's tips)

For the pastry
200g/7oz plain flour
25g/1oz ground almonds
grated zest and juice of 1 medium orange
150g/5oz butter
flour, for dusting

For the filling
225g/8oz boozy mincemeat (see page 192)
1 egg white, lightly beaten
demerara sugar, for sprinkling
edible gold glitter (optional) or sieved
   icing sugar, to decorate
clotted cream or rum butter, to serve
   (optional)

Preheat the oven 190°C/fan oven 170°C/gas mark 5. **Aga 4/3-door** *Top of baking oven.* **Aga 2-door** *Grid shelf on floor of roasting oven.*

Make the pastry by putting all the ingredients, except the orange juice, into a food processor and whizz until it resembles breadcrumbs. Now add 3 tablespoons of the orange juice and whizz until the dough comes together into a ball. Remove, wrap in clingfilm and leave to chill in the fridge for 1 hour.

Roll out two-thirds of the pastry on a floured board to a 3mm/$\frac{1}{8}$ inch thickness. Cut 12 circles out with a 7.5–9cm/3–3$\frac{1}{2}$-inch fluted cutter. Gently press these into the holes of a 12-hole patty tin. The pastry should protrude above the holes slightly to allow for shrinkage when cooked. Spoon a little mincemeat into each pastry case, but don't overfill them.

Add any pastry trimmings to the remaining pastry and roll it out on the floured board. Using a 6cm/2$\frac{1}{2}$-inch star shaped cutter, cut 12 stars out. Press the stars on top of the mincemeat. Brush the stars with the egg white and sprinkle with a little demerara sugar.

Bake the pies for about 15–20 minutes. You might need to turn the patty tin half way through cooking to ensure the pies brown evenly. Leave in the tins for 5 minutes, and then transfer to a wire rack to cool.

Sprinkle with some gold edible glitter or if you are not using it, dust the pies with some icing sugar.

Serve warm, with a good dollop of rum butter or cream.

Lotte's tips
This amount of pastry makes 12 on the initial rolling, including the stars. You can roll out the trimmings and get another 8–9 mince pies with stars on a second rolling and this should take about another 175g/6oz mincemeat.

elizabethan chicken in spiced red wine with plums and orange

This is a recipe that shouldn't work really as it goes against all modern ideas. Red wine, heavy spices and orange cooked with chicken? Surely not. Well, the Elizabethans liked these flavours and so do I – and so do all the various friends I've cooked this for over the years – unless of course they were lying. In which case they can forget their signed copy of this book! If you make it a day in advance, the flavours will intensify. I have frozen this dish too with and without the plums. Both ways are fine, but the plums may be a little squishy once frozen. To be honest though, once heated up, it doesn't make a lot of difference.

Serves 4

For the marinade
425ml/15fl oz red wine
grated zest and juice of 1 large orange
2 cloves
110g/4oz raisins
1 teaspoon ground ginger
$\frac{1}{2}$ teaspoon ground cinnamon
$\frac{1}{4}$ teaspoon freshly grated nutmeg
10 juniper berries

For the casserole
4 large free-range chicken legs, skinned or 4 large free-range boneless, skinless chicken breasts
50g/2oz butter
1 large onion, finely chopped
425ml/15fl oz chicken stock
sprig of fresh rosemary
700g/1$\frac{1}{2}$lb firm plums, halved and stoned
25g/1oz plain flour
2 teaspoons clear honey

salt and freshly ground black pepper
Saffron mash (see opposite) and steamed greens, to serve

To make the marinade, place the red wine, orange zest and juice, cloves, raisins, ginger, cinnamon, and nutmeg in a large jug, stir well. Pinch the juniper berries between your fingers to release their flavour and add to the marinade.

Place the chicken legs or breasts in a shallow, non-metallic container and pour the marinade over. Cover and set aside to marinate in the fridge overnight.

The next day, melt half the butter in a large, non-stick deep sauté pan or a flameproof casserole dish and gently fry the onion until it is soft, about 5 minutes. Add the chicken stock and bring up to boiling point. Simmer for 3 minutes.

Add the chicken, marinade and rosemary sprig, cover and leave to simmer for 20 minutes over a gently heat. Add the plums and continue to cook for a further 10–20 minutes over a gentle heat, until the chicken is thoroughly cooked. To check that the chicken is cooked, carefully pull the largest breast apart, it should be white and opaque inside and not pink.

Preheat the oven to 150°C/fan oven 130°C/gas mark 2. **Aga 4/3/2-door** *Simmering oven.*

Place the remaining butter in a small bowl and add the flour, mash them together with a fork until a smooth paste forms. Set aside.

When cooked, remove the chicken from the pan and place it on a baking tray, and if you can the plums (they may have broken down too much), and keep warm in the oven. Turn up the heat and bubble away for 5 minutes to reduce the sauce a little in order to concentrate the flavour. Add the honey to the pan and stir well.

Use the paste to thicken the sauce (see Lotte's tips). Add a little of the paste at a time, on a whisk, and beat it in as you bring the sauce back up to the boil. As it boils the flour will thicken it. Don't make the sauce too thick. However, if you do overdo it with the paste, just add a little chicken stock or water to let it down again. You don't want a sauce that could set the foundations of a house! It should be glossy and pourable. Season with salt and pepper to taste.

Return the chicken and plums to the pan and serve with Saffron mash and steamed greens. Together, the colours look amazing on the plate!

Lotte's tips
Using a flour and butter paste is an excellent way to thicken a sauce at the end of the cooking time. Make the paste and keep it in a plastic container in the fridge for up to 10 days, to use for other dishes.

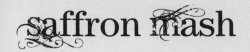
saffron mash

I've been making this for many, many years. The bright egg yolk yellow and the honey fragrance of saffron are beautiful in potato and fabulous paired up with the Elizabethan chicken (see opposite) And the really good thing about this mash is that it freezes! Make a couple of batches, use one and freeze the other (see Lotte's tips).

Serves 6

900g/2lb potatoes (I like Maris Piper or
   King Edward), peeled and diced
pinch of saffron strands
5 tablespoons semi-skimmed milk
5 tablespoons double cream
50g/2oz butter
salt and freshly ground black pepper

Pop the potatoes into a large pan of salted cold water. Bring to the boil and simmer until they are tender.

Steep the saffron in 1 tablespoon of boiling water for 10 minutes.

Heat the milk, cream and saffron together in a small saucepan until boiling, then remove from the heat.

When the potatoes are cooked, drain and return them to the pan. Place the pan back over a gentle heat and shake the potatoes so they dry off and any excess moisture evaporates.

Mash the potatoes with the butter. Gently reheat the saffron mixture over a low heat and beat it into the potatoes Season with salt and pepper.

Lotte's tips
To freeze the mash, set it aside to cool. Spoon the cold mash into freezer bags or a plastic container to freeze. To defrost the mash, place it in the fridge overnight. To reheat the mash pour 2 tablespoons semi-skimmed milk into a medium saucepan and add the potato, heat through very gently, stirring all the time with a wooden spoon until piping hot.

apple and mincemeat frangipane tart with soured cream pastry

My mincemeat makes another entrance here with a perfect pud to serve over Christmas time. You can prepare it the day before if you want and keep it in the fridge – all you have to do the next day is cook and serve. I often make a couple of batches of this soured cream pastry, use one and freeze the other. It freezes beautifully and you'll always have some to hand. Simply defrost it in the fridge overnight and it's ready to use. I insist you give this one a try. It's so easy and full of everything Christmas.

Serves 6–8

For the pastry
175g/6oz plain flour
150g/5oz unsalted butter, cubed and chilled
7 tablespoons soured cream
flour, for dusting

For the filling
2 dessert apples, cored and sliced
juice of 1 lemon
50g/2oz butter, softened
50g/2oz golden caster sugar
2 eggs, lightly beaten
110g/4oz ground almonds
3–4 drops almond extract
4 tablespoons Boozy mincemeat (see page 192)
3–4 tablespoons apricot jam or Winter tonic jelly (see page 158), to glaze
cream or ice cream, to serve

Preheat the oven to 200°C/fan oven 180°C.gas mark 6. **Aga 4/3/2-door** *Grid shelf on the floor of the roasting oven*

Line a large baking sheet with baking parchment.

Make the pastry by placing the flour into a food processor with the cubed and chilled butter. Whizz until it resembles breadcrumbs. Add the soured cream and whizz until it just comes together. Turn onto a floured surface and gently knead until a dough is formed. Wrap the dough in clingfilm and chill in the fridge for 1 hour.

For the filling, toss the apples in the lemon juice.

Place the butter and sugar in a medium mixing bowl and beat them together with a wooden spoon until they are light and fluffy. Gradually beat in the eggs and then stir in the ground almonds. Add the almond extract, cover and set aside.

Roll the pastry out onto a lightly floured surface to a 30cm/12 inch circle, then transfer it to the lined baking sheet and prick all over with a fork.

Spread the mincemeat over the centre of the pastry leaving a border of about 4cm/1$\frac{1}{2}$ inches around the edge. Spread the almond mixture on top of the mincemeat.

Arrange the sliced apples around and on top of the frangipane. Then fold about 2$\frac{1}{2}$cm/1 inch of the pastry into the centre, over the fruit. Chill in the fridge for 20 minutes.

Bake for 30–40 minutes until golden brown. If it is browning a bit too much towards the end of the cooking time, cover the tart with foil.

Leave the tart on the baking sheet for 10 minutes before carefully sliding it onto a serving dish.

Place the apricot jam or Winter tonic jelly in a small pan and gently warm it over a low heat. Brush the melted jam or jelly all over the top of the tart, including the pastry. This tart is equally delicious served hot, warm or cold but must be devoured with lashings of cream or ice cream!

mr darcy's pink glittery macaroons

**Darcy's Large Pile,
Shropshire**

My dearest Fanny,

As I sit here composing this letter to you my dear, I am enticing Mr Darcy with his favourite sweetmeat. I own in fact to being his first and most desired sweetmeat; with these delicate little macaroons adorned with the finest shining glitter, his second.

We have spent most of Christmastide wrapped in each other's arms and I do declare to being so in love it pains me.

It is wonderful indeed that I have found love at my time in life. I thought spinsterhood would be mine, now that age has destroyed my youthful bloom. Oh, Darcy has revived my spirit, and I confess revived other parts of me that I thought not existed.

I know my happiness is important to you Fanny, and I can oblige your concerns with nothing more than love in its most innocent and purest form. Darcy is my life now, but I miss you terribly. Your wit and humour.

Oh, sister, there is another who longs for your company.

Lord Dashwood is so taken with yourself. I do declare that he spends most of his days with your small miniature clutched to his breast. He longs for you to agree to his hand in marriage. I have knowledge of your love for him; I say consider his marriage... and large fortune. To refuse would be such folly.

Fanny dear, return to your sister and come and live with us amongst the rolling hills of Shropshire. I am lonely on the days that Darcy visits his estates.

Miss Honey is my only companion at these times and I fancy that a round cat with ginger complexion and a fondness for her own rodent sweetmeats does not fulfil my thirst for conversation.

And Darcy does jest her size so, it makes me terribly vexed. Thankfully Miss Honey doesn't seem to notice the tease; otherwise I fear another march on her territory.

We could have much fun. I imagine us, laughing as we take a turn of the gardens after supper, gossiping as we used to. My time with needlepoint is dull indeed without Fanny there to offer her advice. Your letters from town are not enough to inspire.

Please accept Lord Dashwood's offer of marriage with no more delay. I earnestly press your coming to us.

As ever,

Your sister Martha

These keep for a few days in an airtight container and are fabulous alongside a mince pie or two for tea, or as a pressie.

**Makes 24 petit-four size or
12 larger, tea-time size**

rice paper, to line 2 baking sheets
150g/5oz ground almonds
150g/5oz caster sugar
1½ teaspoons ground rice
2 egg whites
a few drops of pink food colouring
½ teaspoon almond extract
24 or 12 whole blanched almonds
   (depending on which size you make)
edible glitter, to decorate

Preheat the oven to 180°C/fan oven 160°C/gas mark 4. **Aga 4/3-door** *Middle of baking oven.* **Aga 2-door** *Grid shelf on floor of roasting oven with cold plain shelf on second runners.*

Line 2 baking sheets with rice paper.

Place the ground almonds, sugar and ground rice into a medium mixing bowl. Add the egg whites and mix well. Now add enough food colouring to give the macaroons a nice strong pink colour. Stir in the almond extract.

Put heaped teaspoonfuls (for the petit-four size) or dessertspoonfuls (for the tea-time size) of the almond mixture in your hand and roll into balls. Place, spaced well apart, on the rice paper. Flatten the balls slightly and press an almond onto the top of each one.

Bake in the oven for about 10 minutes, but do check they aren't getting too brown half way through, and if they are, just loosely cover them with foil. Remove from the oven and cool on a wire rack. At this point, while the macaroons are still warm, sprinkle some edible glitter on them.

Break off and discard the excess rice paper from around the edges of the macaroons and enjoy!

cidered pea and ham soup

This soup is made, without fail every Boxing day. I keep the apple juice and cider stock that the Christmas ham has been cooked in, cool it and remove the fat and then I toss in some dried peas and any leftover ham. If there are any forlorn and lonely sprouts in the fridge, or a glazed carrot or two – they are encouraged to join the soup party. I finish it off with some double cream (one year with brandy cream from the pudding – actually rather splendid!) and then tell myself it's doing me the world of good and the diet will eventually start tomorrow... This dish really is the bed-sock of the soup world. Thick, warming and just a little bit fluffy.

Serves 4

apple and cider stock with vegetables, from Christmas baked ham, page 206 (cooled overnight in the fridge)
275g/10oz split yellow peas
approximately 225g/8oz leftover ham, finely chopped
150ml/5fl oz double cream
freshly ground black pepper
extra cream (optional), to garnish
warm bread, to serve

Remove the white fat from the top of the stock and discard it.

Heat the stock and vegetables up in a large saucepan and add the split peas. Bring to the boil, cover and simmer for 2–2½ hours or until the peas are soft and fall apart when pressed against the edge of the pan with a spoon.

Transfer the soup to a blender or food processor and blend it until it is smooth. Return to the pan.

Add the ham to the soup with the double cream and heat until piping hot. Season with some black pepper, you'll find you've no need for any salt.

Serve with some warm bread and perhaps a little more cream swirled on top.

chocolate mess

Caroline, one of the Hussys, had a party many years ago and asked me to bring a pudding. I cobbled together some ingredients I had left over from a children's party (obviously NOT the rum!) and came up with this. It was named Chocolate mess on the night, perhaps because it's not the prettiest of puddings. What it is though, is a tribute to storecupboard ingredients and the ability to make grown men weep with joy when they eat it! As it's so quick to make, you don't really need to assemble it in advance but it will keep quite happily for a couple of hours if you want to be organised and make it ahead of time.

Serves 8

200g/7oz dark chocolate, broken into
    pieces
200g/7oz milk chocolate, broken into
    pieces
1kg carton readymade (county next to
    Cornwall!) custard
250g bag amaretti biscuits, crushed
4 tablespoons dark rum, amaretto or
    Tia Maria (optional)
570ml/1 pint double cream
2 milk chocolate flakes, broken up

Place the dark and milk chocolate pieces in a heatproof bowl and melt it in the microwave or over a pan of simmering water. Leave to cool for 5 minutes.

Tip the custard into a medium mixing bowl. Stir in the melted chocolate and mix well.

Place half the crushed amaretti biscuits in the bottom of a 1.7 litre/3 pint glass serving dish. Drizzle with half the alcohol, if using.

Pour half the chocolate custard over the top. Add another layer of crushed biscuits (reserving a few for the top), more rum and then the rest of the custard.

Lightly whip the cream to the same consistency as the custard. Using a large metal spoon, gently fold half the crushed chocolate flakes into the cream. Spoon this over the custard.

Sprinkle with the remaining chocolate flakes and the remaining crushed amaretti biscuits.

Lotte's tips
I think this pudding makes a great alternative to trifle at Christmas. When I brought this to the party, Caroline thought it had a whole host of exotic ingredients in it, and it was a complicated mousse-like dessert. I kept the aura of mystery around it for a few months, until I finally caved in and told the truth!

potted stilton with apple and warm pear and cranberry chutney

One year, as usual I had the ubiquitous leftover Stilton cheese sitting in my larder. You know what it's like – you buy too much in the pre-Christmas shopping fest and then you're left with the stinky stuff and no real desire to eat it. I hate waste and rarely chuck anything away. My fridge is testament to this. So I did what hundreds of sensible cooks have done before me – potted the beggar! Mixed with some apple, livened up with some lemon and softened by cream, potted Stilton made it into my top ten favourite dishes. It's completely scrumptious with this warm pear and cranberry chutney (which is also wonderful alongside hot or cold meats), served on a crisp cracker and with a large glass of rich red wine.

Serves 4

350g/12oz Stilton cheese
1 large dessert apple, peeled
1 small cooking apple, peeled
grated zest and juice of $\frac{1}{2}$ lemon
5 tablespoons single cream
freshly ground black pepper
warm bread rolls or crackers and
    Pear and cranberry chutney, to serve
    (see below)

Crumble the Stilton into a medium mixing bowl.

Grate both apples onto the Stilton. Add the lemon zest and juice and stir well to prevent the apples from browning. Add the cream and season with a little black pepper. Mix well.

Spoon the mixture into a serving dish and serve with crackers or spread it on some squidgy warm bread rolls and serve with Pear and cranberry chutney.

Lotte's tips
This lasts for a week in the fridge if you seal the surface with some clarified butter (see page 62).

If you still have some Stilton left over, freeze it in portions and use if for Cauliflower soup with melted Stilton (see page 31).

Pear and cranberry chutney

Serves 4

50g/2oz butter
1 medium red onion, chopped
450g/1lb pears, peeled, cored and diced
175g/6oz seedless raisins
1 teaspoon mixed spice
2 tablespoons balsamic vinegar
1 tablespoon cider vinegar
5 tablespoons dark brown sugar
225g/8oz cranberries
grated zest and juice of 1 large orange
4 tablespoons port
salt and freshly ground black pepper

Melt the butter in a medium saucepan and cook the onion gently over a low heat for 5 minutes until soft.

Add the pears and raisins and cook for 10 minutes.

Add the mixed spice, vinegars, sugar, cranberries, orange zest and juice and port, stir well and cook for another 10 minutes or so.

Season with a little salt and pepper. Taste and then add more sugar or vinegar to your own taste – it may need some more, or you may be bang on! This is best served warm.

If you are not using the chutney straight away, transfer it to a lidded plastic container and store in the fridge for up to 10 days. Heat through gently before serving.

Lotte's tips
This goes beautifully with the turkey on Christmas day – I also use it to eat with cold ham the next day.

baked christmas ham with a sugar and mustard glaze

Now, I think this is a scrummy dish to cook for friends and family on Christmas Eve. Serve it hot with some Saffron mash (see page 197), Plum and ginger chutney (see page 209) and some steamed green veg. Then eat it cold over the next few days. In doughy bread sandwiches with mustard or next to a fluffy baked potato with some more chutney and perhaps some coleslaw. I've cooked many hams over the years, in many different ways, but I always come back to this recipe of mine – it is the best.

Serves 8

1.8kg/4lb uncooked gammon joint
   (ask your butcher if it needs soaking
   overnight in cold water)
1 litre/1^3/$_4$ pint medium dry cider
1 litre/1^3/$_4$ pint clear apple juice
1 large onion, cut into chunks
2 stalks celery, cut into chunks
4 carrots, cut into chunks
2 bay leaves
20 cloves
75g/3oz butter, softened
175g/6oz dark brown muscovado sugar
1 teaspoon English mustard
1 tablespoon Dijon mustard
1 teaspoon ground ginger
1 teaspoon ground cloves
1 teaspoon ground cinnamon
Saffron mash, Plum and ginger chutney
   and steamed greens, to serve

Preheat the oven to 220˚C/fan oven 200˚C/gas mark 7. **Aga 4/3/2-door** *Lower roasting oven.*

If you have soaked the gammon, drain it and place it skin side up in a large saucepan. Pour in the cider and apple juice and add the onion, celery, carrot and bay leaves. Bring up to the boil, cover and simmer for 1^1/$_2$ hours.

Remove the joint from the pan, peel off the skin with a knife (discard or give to the birds in the garden, they love it!) and use a sharp knife to score the fat in a diagonal pattern. Reserve the stock to use for the Cidered pea and ham soup (see page 201). Don't strain, just leave it to cool with the vegetables in it. Stand the gammon in a roasting tin lined with foil. Stud the diamonds of fat with the cloves.

Place the butter, sugar, mustards and spices in a medium mixing bowl and mix well to form a paste. Spread the paste over the fat. Roast the ham in the oven for about 20 minutes, basting twice during this time.

Roast for another 5–10 minutes then remove from the oven and keep basting it as the sticky sauce cools. As it does the sugar starts to solidify and it will start to stick and stay to the top of the ham. Continue until as much as of the syrup as possible is on the ham. I don't want you to worry, it will get quite toffee like and that is exactly what you want.

Remove from the roasting tin and place on a serving dish. Carve at the table or quietly in the kitchen with no-one watching – always best as you can sneak a mouthful or two in before anyone else! Serve some Plum and ginger chutney on the side and if this is a Christmas Eve supper, perhaps some Saffron mash and steamed greens.

Lotte's tips
The cooked ham freezes well. I always think it's best to freeze it in portions (a couple of slices each). Wrap in greaseproof paper and then foil, making sure you include some of the delicious sticky saucy topping. Thaw overnight in the fridge to defrost thoroughly. You can either reheat the defrosted ham by frying it in a little butter until it is piping hot or eat it cold.

my famous (and-now-no-longer-secret) curried sausage rolls

This recipe used to be very secret. Only a few had the recipe, and then they had to run the gauntlet and bestow great riches at my feet to get it. Some fought for it, some tried blackmail – and all you had to do was buy my book – I think you got off rather lightly! On a more sensible note, I really do make these every year without fail. Everyone who has come across these naughty little rolls has fallen in love with them. can't blame them at all – the spiced sausage nestled amongst layers of buttery pastry is enough to get the most hardened culinary cynic weeping for more. Make and freeze by the hundredweight – you'll eat them all, I promise!

Makes approximately 35

2 tablespoons rapeseed oil
1 medium onion, finely chopped
3 garlic cloves, crushed
1 teaspoon chilli powder
1 teaspoon ground cumin
1 teaspoon ground coriander
1 teaspoon ground turmeric
150ml/5fl oz red wine
juice of 1/2 lemon
700g/11/2lb good-quality sausagemeat
    (Musks is my favourite)
flour, for dusting
500g packet puff pastry
1 egg, beaten

Preheat the oven to 200°C/fan oven 180°C/gas mark 6. **Aga 4/3/2-door** *Grid shelf on floor of roasting oven.*

Heat the oil in a large, non-stick frying pan and add the onion and garlic, cook gently until soft, for about 5 minutes.

Now, add the spices and cook for a minute or so to release the flavour and oils. Pour in the red wine and let it bubble away and reduce for a couple of minutes to about 2 tablespoons full. Remove from the heat, add the lemon juice and leave to cool.

Place the sausagemeat in a medium bowl, add the cooled spice mixture and mix well.

On a floured worksurface, roll out the pastry to a rectangle, 40x60cm/16x24 inches, the pastry should be about 3mm/1/8 inch thick. The longer edge should be the closest edge to you.

Brush about 7.5cm/3 inches of the longer edge of the pastry, closest to you, with the beaten egg.

Flour your hands and make a 60cm/ 24 inch long sausage with the meat mixture and lay it across the pastry, about 21/2cm/1 inch from the edge. Pull the edge of the pastry over the sausage and press the edges of the pastry firmly together.

Cut the pastry with the wrapped sausage, in half, and carefully roll each piece to make sure the edges are stuck together.

Cut both rolls into individual sausage rolls, using a sharp knife, the size is up to you, but I prefer ones about 5cm/ 2 inches long. Place on non-stick baking sheets.

Snip each roll twice with scissors, (the cut will look like a 'v'), brush with beaten egg and cook in the oven for about 10–15 minutes or until golden brown and cooked through. Transfer to a wire rack to cool.

Add a bit of Christmassy sparkle to your party...

This has got to be the best ever drink to serve with the curried sausage rolls or for that matter, any nibbly bits and pieces! Dip a sugar lump in a small amount of red food colouring (not too much; you only want the drink to be pink) and drop it in a Champagne flute.

Sprinkle over some fairy dust... er, sorry, edible glitter, and then top up with some chilled cava or Champagne.

Cheers!

warm plum and ginger chutney

My final quick warm chutney – as with all the others dotted amongst the pages of this book – it's delicious with cold ham, beef, cheese, pâté and even a curry.

Serves 8–10

25g/1oz butter
1 large onion, chopped
450g/1lb plums, quartered, stoned and
    roughly chopped
2 teaspoons grated fresh ginger
2 tablespoons balsamic vinegar, or to
    taste
1 tablespoon soft brown sugar, or to
    taste

Melt the butter in a medium saucepan, over a medium heat, and add the onion. Gently fry for 5 minutes. Add the plums and ginger, cover and cook gently for 10 minutes or until the plums are soft. If the plums are not very juicy, by all means add 3 tablespoons cold water.

Add the balsamic vinegar and sugar. As with my other quick chutneys, you want an even sweet-sour taste, and as the sweetness of plums varies add the vinegar and sugar gradually until you get the required taste. Serve warm.

If you are not using the chutney straight away, transfer it to a lidded plastic container and store in the fridge for up to 10 days. Heat through gently before serving.

slow roasted shoulder of pork rebellion in cider

You'll notice that there isn't a recipe for Lotte's traditional family turkey in here. Well the reason is (between you and me) turkey's just not my favourite. Of course I've cooked it on TV and at home for many years (my dad loves it), but given the chance I'd rather have some beef or this recipe. When I cooked it last year, I almost had pre-Christmas mutiny on my hands. I couldn't convince anyone that it was a good idea to have this terribly easy and rather yummy dish to eat. They didn't think Christmas would be the same without a turkey. The day wouldn't feel right, the world would end, blah, blah, blah. What a lot of people forget if they aren't actually cooking the lunch, is the fact that it's an awful lot of work for one day. Turkey with the trimmings can be hugely time consuming and people get so worried about how to cook it. Every year I get asked the best way, how not to get stressed, how to do the Brussels, which stuffing is best – that sort of thing. Every year my usual reply is to start on the sherry early – I find it usually removes all forms of stress! But last year, I thought I'm going to take the bull by the horns and refuse to cook a turkey. I was going to serve pork up to my family whether they liked it or not. The reason? I was tired. I'd been working like a Trojan in the weeks before, and I wanted to enjoy Christmas day and not be found face down in the stuffing through exhaustion. So, with much muttering from everyone seated around the table, I brought out the pork. They soon shut up – it was tender, moist and utterly delicious. The crackling perched on top was perfection itself.

I served it with some goose fat roasted potatoes, parsnips, the inevitable Brussels, and a cauliflower cheese. It was the easiest Christmas lunch I've ever cooked and possibly the most scrumptious. I almost had a rebellion, but I quelled it successfully and next year I'm going to do the same. Not for me hours of basting and stuffing. I'm going to put the pork into the oven and then sit down, relax and enjoy time with my family.

Serves 8

1.8kg/4lb rolled boneless pork shoulder
  joint
2 teaspoon dried thyme
2 tablespoons rapeseed oil
1 large leek, sliced
570ml/1 pint medium cider
275ml/10fl oz chicken stock
4 garlic cloves, crushed
2 large cooking apples, peeled, cored
  and sliced
1 teaspoon dried sage
1 fresh bay leaf
2 tablespoons chopped fresh parsley
sea salt and freshly ground black pepper

Preheat the oven to 160°C.fan oven 140°C/gas mark 3. **Aga 4/3-door** *Grid shelf on floor of baking oven.* **Aga 2-door** *Grid shelf on floor of roasting oven with cold plain shelf on third runners. (I usually start the pork off in the baking/roasting oven then continue most of the cooking in the simmering oven.)*

Cut the rind off the pork and score with a sharp knife. Set aside.

Rub a little sea salt over the rolled pork and sprinkle with the dried thyme. Heat the oil in a large flameproof casserole dish over a medium heat and brown the pork all over. Scatter over the leek and pour over the cider and stock. Stir in the garlic, the sliced apples and then tuck the herbs down under the liquid. Bring up to the boil, then cover and place in the oven for 4 hours, turning half-way through.

Take the rind and place on a baking sheet. Rub some salt into the skin and lay it skin side up. Place in oven and cook for 4 hours too.

After the 4 hours, remove the pork from the liquid, cover it with foil and leave it to rest for 20–30 minutes somewhere warm.

Increase the oven temperature to 240°C/fan oven 220°C/gas mark 9 and crisp up the crackling. **Aga 4/3/2-door** *Top of roasting oven. This will take about 10–15 minutes.*

Bring the pork cooking liquor to the boil to reduce it by one-third and season to taste. All the apples will be pulped down and the flavours intensified. Skim off any fat that rises to the surface.

Slice the pork (it should just fall apart) and serve with some crackling, the apple gravy on top and on the side, and plenty of Christmas good tidings – go on, you know you can!

Darcy's Large Pile, Shropshire

Dearest Fanny,

I am sad not to have heard from you since you eloped with Lord Dashwood, and I do hope this missive finds you both well.

I own to being quite astonished by this sudden decision on your part, but knowing the unconquerable power of love – and lust, (a knowledge I fancy I am now fully aware of) I am not surprised.

I fear Miss Honey may never recover from her disappointment though. She was so looking forward to receiving the honour of maiden on your wedding day. There has been much amusement on my part.

I have been highly diverted at the possibility of Miss Honey in lace and finery. A bonnet would have rendered me incapable of speech and dear Darcy paralysed with humour.

I own that Miss Honey may have found purchasing such a garment in Shropshire great pleasure, but an enormous frustration. After all, I have hesitation in imagining that they make bonnets outside London with tiny holes for ears?

I have gossip. A carriage of quality arrived today. Aboard this monstrous beast were seated Lord and Lady Saunders. It was too great a shock to be borne of composure my dear, I am afraid I was on the verge of hysteria, with palpitations of such enormity that I took to my bed.

Darling Darcy had to entertain them for I feared for my conversation.

They declared they had called on me to apologise for their misdemeanour. How they can own that removing the finest cook in the land from my employ as a small transgression, is far beyond reasonable behaviour.

Sister, I stayed within the confines of my rooms. I could not bring myself to speak to them. Such disagreeable characters; with bad humour, and an ability to pilfer cooks from under your nose.

They left after taking some tea, Darcy ever the gentlemen entertained them for almost an hour. I, on the other hand had pricked my finger during some cross moments with my needlepoint, in the confines of my parlour. Melancholy had set its sight on me sister, but Darcy has a way of lifting my spirits. I do not suppose that I could love a man more.

So, dearest Fanny, Christmastide is almost at an end, and I still long for a visit from Lord and Lady Dashwood. Oh, that name suggests such fine character. Please do make haste to our door, you will find friends here and we look forward to welcoming you both. We will open the cellar for our dear friends with much aplomb – I fancy that you and I may enjoy a glass or two of claret, and will emit an air of sweet radiance that both our husbands will agree are our finest attributes.

Write soon.
With dearest affection
Martha (Darcy)

thank you

There are many, many people who have influenced and helped me over the years, both in the kitchen and out. My parents obviously – I was very lucky to have a wonderful upbringing by two marvellous individuals who loved me, cuddled me, and made me the balanced person I am today.

My Father: witty, artistic and utterly reliable. He will always remain the most important man in my life. A man, who I unquestionably look up to and admire. (www.duncancartoons.com)

My Mother: a fabulous, cosy homemaker and cook who influenced and nurtured my ability to build a nest. A bit nutty and a very funny actress who trod the boards both professional and amateur. I miss her terribly.

My wonderful Daisy. We were brought together when I was only 22 and to some extent we have grown up together. My life would not be as fulfilled, bountiful and downright fabulous without her. She won't follow me into the professional kitchen. However I secretly know she has developed a small love of cooking (although she may not admit it), and this will enable her to feed and nourish herself and her future family with flourish. I really couldn't ask for more.

Delia – a very easy target for some television chefs, but one of my first culinary influences and her books always made up the cookery prizes I was awarded on many occasions at school. Her Summer Collection is still one of my favourites. I like Delia. So there!

Agent Annie – she's my agent and she's called Annie! She has been my agent for six years and has really had faith in me when others haven't. It's hard working in my world. You're turned down for jobs more times in a year, than most people would get in a lifetime. You learn not to care and say it's water off a duck's back. But in reality you do need a day or two to lick your wounds, mourn the job and carry on.

It's easy as an agent to harden to bad news and perhaps not deliver it to your client in the most sympathetic manner. But Annie is sensitive, kind and understands and she happens to get me some fabulous jobs too. When she needs to be (and this is the reason you have an agent), she can kick some butt and protect your interests as only a lioness protecting her cubs can. I love Agent Annie – she's the best. Not only my agent, but a wonderful friend, too.

Now, here are a few of the lovelies who helped me with this book. I penned an e-mail asking if they would kindly test my recipes. All but three or four are non-professional cooks. It was important to me to get the opinions of home cooks, because this is the style of food I cook. 'Be honest' I said, 'I require your thoughts on how easy or difficult you found them, if they tasted good and if they were easy to read and understand'.

I may have found some of the honesty a bit uncomfortable, (only because I have leanings towards being a control freak!) but their opinions were right and without their input, these recipes wouldn't be half as good. So a really big thank you and big kisses to:

Chloe Bellars, Thomas Bellars, Jane Bellars, Caroline Brown, Simon Brown, Sian Bush-Cavel, Jacqueline Coopey, Louise Cope, Doddie (Lissie Mead), Nicky Donnelly, The Duchess of Cork (Margaret Browne), Sarah Durdin-Robertson, Annabel Hartog, Elizabeth Hayward, Amanda Hollyer, Miranda Hollyer, Sandra Kitashima, Caroline McLeod, Gilli McWilliams, Julia Oldham, Jennie Phillipps, Craig Rowe, Sarah Scott, Cat Sheppard, Robyn Stevens Jaq Supple, Sally Thompson, Sue Tiplady, Chrissie Walker, Phoebe Weiland and Eleanor and all the lovely ladies at Violet's Pantry who tested my recipes, and gave me their opinions on the forum (www.violetspantry.forumup.org).

Absolute Press and all who sail with her. Jon Croft, publisher and rather clever man – he read a bit of my blog, bought me lunch and decided there and then that he would publish my book. At this first meeting, over delicious food and much wine, Jon really did understand exactly where I was coming from. He 'got' me. Obviously a man with great clarity and instinct! Thank you Jon, for this amazing opportunity, I've enjoyed every moment of it. Absolute Press are a dream to work with. Matt Inwood, Art Director and another very clever man. Like Jon, he understood me, my cooking style and life very quickly. He has transformed my ideas, writing and the photography into a beautiful book that truly encompasses what I am all about. He has also been a complete pleasure to work with, makes me laugh with very silly emails and has a secret talent that he tries to keep quiet – he is very good at washing up. Big thank you also to Elizabeth of Mar, Claire Siggery, Meg Avent, Andrea O'Connor and everyone else involved with, and part of the fabulous Absolute Press.

Lovely Lara Loo (Holmes), Photographer. We've spent an awful lot of time together over this last year photographing my food, house, garden – and cats! Lara's gentle nature and kind personality veils an utterly professional work ethic and an eye for spectacular photography. She has transformed my cottage and gardens into a magical sparkly world and made my food look simply stunning. Thank you Lara Loo – you are the best.

Jane Bamforth, Editor. I've never had my recipes edited before. I thought everyone would know what I meant if I wrote 'milk' instead of 'semi skimmed' and 'flour' instead of 'plain flour'. Apparently not! This was just the first lesson I learnt from Jane. The others were 'non-stick' pans or not, wooden spoons or whisk and how many does that recipe serve or make? Jane obviously did a lot more than the above to make my ramblings coherent and complete and for that I am enormously grateful. Thank you Jane, for, like everyone else, understanding me completely and editing me so well.

And finally (yes really) enormous thanks to all of you reading this – for buying my book you have ensured that my cats will continue to be well fed. They are eternally grateful.